CLAUDIA & DOMINICA
TOO DELICIOUS

Claudia Shaw-d'Auriol & Dominica Yang

HAVEN
BOOKS

Thank you to the following people: To our respective husbands, Guy and Trevor, and our wonderful families for their unquestioning support and love. To Danielle Huthart for her continued creative direction and dedication. Our thanks also to Dania Shawwa Abuali and Liz Lee from Haven Books, Robin Fern and Room to Read, Susan Jung for her support, Vivian Herijanto, Bambine Wise, Tara Jenkins, Karen Pittar and Patrick Poon.

Just as in our first book, DELICIOUS, this cookbook could not have been possible without some best-loved recipes passed on to us from friends and family, and without the countless sources of culinary inspiration on which we have relied over the years. We have both enjoyed long love affairs with wonderful cookbooks and cookery magazines, from *Gourmet, Vogue Entertaining* and *House & Garden*, to Martha Stewart, Delia Smith, Gary Rhodes, and believe it or not, a really old Penguin cookery book. These have all given us a starting point for years of domestic culinary adventures as we fed our loved ones and planned dinner parties. As cooking is our passion, and not our profession, we cannot take all the credit for all of the recipes in these pages, although many were indeed created in our very own kitchens. Our aim is to share our top family favourites and our tried-and-tested entertaining staples, some of which are interpretations of existing popular recipes shared amongst friends.

Published in Hong Kong by Haven Books Limited

ISBN 978-988-98819-9-3

Copyright © 2008 Claudia Shaw-d'Auriol and Dominica Yang

Art direction and design by Whitespace

Food styling by Vivian Herijanto at Corner Kitchen

Photography by Patrick Poon, C.C. Lam and Tango Chan at Koji Studio

Proceeds from the sale of this book will benefit Room to Read (www.roomtoread.org)

Cover recipes:
on left — Spicy Chicken with Basil (page 23)
on right — Roast Peaches wiith Caramel Sauce (page 126)

This book is typeset in Trade Gothic.
Printed in Hong Kong by Handsome Printing Ltd.

www.havenbooksonline.com
www.whitespace.hk
www.claudiaanddominica.com

CLAUDIA & DOMINICA
TOO DELICIOUS

Proceeds from this book will be donated to Room to Read, a charity that provides books, schools, libraries and girls scholarships to children across the developing world.

We wanted the proceeds from our second book to benefit an international charity where our contribution would have a truly positive impact. Room to Read was the perfect choice; a charity that provides underprivileged children with the same opportunities as those in the developed world. We admired their energy, their organisation and their unstinting commitment to education. We are thrilled at the opportunity to work with Room to Read, with whom we can share the fruits of our efforts with the many needy children out there who have a passion to learn. In a sense we have created a book to provide books!

Room to Read (www.roomtoread.org) partners with local communities throughout the developing world to provide quality educational opportunities by establishing libraries, creating local language children's literature, constructing schools, providing education to girls and establishing computer labs. We seek to intervene early in the lives of children in the belief that education empowers people to improve socioeconomic conditions for their families, communities, countries and future generations. Through the opportunities that only education can provide, we strive to break the cycle of poverty, one child at a time.

"EDUCATION IS A HUMAN RIGHT WITH IMMENSE POWER TO TRANSFORM. ON ITS FOUNDATION REST THE CORNERSTONES OF FREEDOM, DEMOCRACY AND SUSTAINABLE HUMAN DEVELOPMENT."
Kofi Annan, former Secretary General, the United Nations

Room to Read is impacting lives! With over 1.7 million children accessing over 440 schools, 5,160 bilingual libraries, 226 new local language children's titles, 108 computer labs, and 4,036 girls in our long-term scholarship program — we are providing opportunities that change children's lives and communities throughout the developing world. With your help, we can reach our goal of an additional 5,000 libraries to impact more than 5 million children by 2010.

Room to Read had its humble origins in Nepal in 2000, where we began bringing donated books to rural communities. Today, we are a global organization that helps children gain access to education through a variety of programs. Our libraries give children a friendly space to read and to explore. Our children's books allow students to read in their local language. Our schools give children a safe place to learn. Our scholarships enable girls to enroll in and stay in school. And our computer labs make it possible for children to gain 21st century skills. We currently work in nine countries with plans to expand further throughout Asia, Africa, Latin America and beyond to bring educational opportunities and resources to children throughout the developing world.

Room to Read's programs have reached more than two million children so far. One such student is Thao Pajuay Phankommadam, a young boy from Laos. Thao lives in a remote farming village without electricity or running water. The local school was rundown, and there was no library or books – not even textbooks for the teachers. In 2007 Room to Read established a library in Thao's school, filled with hundreds of books as well as games, puzzles, and posters. Thao told us, "Now I have so many books to read! On weekends I bring books home from school. The children in my neighborhood will come to my house and listen to me tell stories. At night I read the books to my parents, brothers and sisters. Before we received the library, I used to daydream about what it would be like to read books. Now with all of these new books, my dreams have come true."

Imagine a world in which every child has access to an education. Room to Read is doing our best to make this dream a reality, one child at a time. To learn more about our work, visit our website at **www.roomtoread.org**.

Room to Read®

CLAUDIA & DOMINICA
TOO DELICIOUS

Introduction   11

Savoury   16

Sweet   94

Index   183

FRONT

NOTES FROM THE KITCHEN
CLAUDIA DOMINICA

I know for many women cooking is a chore. Fortunately for me, cooking has always been a joy, an adventure. In the confines of my own kitchen, each time I swirl butter into a pan and watch it foam, rub crushed garlic and rosemary onto a rack of lamb, each time I melt chocolate to start a cake, I begin a uniquely rewarding culinary journey that awakens the emotions, electrifies all the senses and evokes vivid memories. Sometimes the journey takes me to the past, such as when I am cooking one of my mother's recipes. Sometimes it transports me to exotic lands, or makes me revisit familiar ones, as when I cook with spices and flavours I first tasted overseas. Sometimes it brings me new friends or cements old friendships, just like the one Dominica and I share. Sometimes it brings my children into the kitchen to dip their fingers into whatever is being made.

No matter the journey, the final destination is always the same: to the heart. In fact, the journey begins and ends in one place, the heart. From mine to my family, my friends and my guests, and from mine to yours.

Because love really is the most important ingredient of all. Cook from the heart and the food will always be DELICIOUS.

Cooking reflects the way we live. Our boys once said, 'Food is life or death!' Food is indeed a passion in our family; meal times are special times. My mother has always been an amazing cook and hostess. I recall numerous dinner parties at home and I loved being a part of it all, folding the napkins, cutting intricate vegetable decorations and of course, tasting the food!

Now a mother of three boys myself, I am continuing the family tradition of making meals the centre of family life; there is so much joy to be shared chatting over a bowl of noodles, indulging in freshly baked chocolate brownies, or sharing a leftover piece of treacle tart. It doesn't matter if the fare is complex, basic or simply just a taste, the result always gives comfort and satisfaction. Savoury or sweet, food brings back good memories, or simply pleases. I love the whole process, from kneading dough, chopping fresh coriander, watching Yorkshire pudding rise to immersing myself in the aroma of cooking!

Claudia and I decided to write a second book because we had so much fun writing the first, and we hope these new recipes bring more happy times to you and your families. Cooking should be fun and if it doesn't work out quite as you expect, improvise and create your own dish! So, put on the apron and start cooking!

SAVOURY

"Food, family, laughter — the perfect recipe!"

Dominica

TORO & GOAT CHEESE DIP

This is a sensational dip — the toro and goat cheese are an insane combination.

240g (8 oz) toro, fresh belly of tuna, finely chopped
180g (6 oz) fresh soft goat cheese, mashed
2 teaspoons finely chopped anchovies
1 tablespoon olive oil
1 tablespoon finely chopped chives
¾ tablespoon Japanese soya sauce
¾ tablespoon *mirin*
½ teaspoon finely chopped garlic
½ teaspoon finely chopped ginger
1 pinch cayenne pepper
1 pinch sea salt
1 pinch white pepper

Garnish
A few stalks of chives, cut in 2.5cm (1 inch) lengths
Thinly cut *nori* (Japanese seaweed)

Mix together all the ingredients except the garnishes. Adjust the seasonings to taste, then spoon into a dip bowl and garnish with the chives and *nori*.

Serve with plain thin crackers or *crudités* — it is magical!

Serves 8

SHANTUNG CHICKEN

Another classic all-time family favourite — easy to prepare and please!

1 medium or 2 small spring chickens
1 teaspoon salt
2 teaspoons five-spice powder
Oil for deep frying
1 ginger slice, minced or finely chopped
4 spring onions, finely chopped
Parsley, to garnish

Seasoning
1 tablespoon dark soya sauce
1 tablespoon Xiao Shing rice wine
½ teaspoon salt
1 tablespoon oil

Remove the innards from the chicken then rinse it inside and out and pat it dry. Rub the salt and five-spice powder thoroughly into the skin and leave for at least 30 minutes.

Heat the wok well, then add the oil for frying. When the oil is very hot, deep fry the chicken over very high heat until the skin turns golden brown on all sides. (If you do not like to deep fry, add enough oil to come halfway up the chicken then keep ladling the boiling oil over the top of the chicken.) If you're cooking two chickens, it's easiest to fry them one at a time.

Transfer the chicken to a shallow dish and drain it to remove the excess oil. Let the chicken cool for 5–10 minutes then rub it with the minced ginger and chopped spring onion.

Mix the seasoning ingredients and pour over the chicken, rubbing it into the skin.

Place the dish in a steamer and steam over moderate heat for 30–40 minutes.

Remove from the steamer, tear the meat from the bones and shred into slivers. Arrange on a bed of shredded lettuce with the skin pieces on the top. Pour the liquid from the steaming dish over the meat and garnish with sprigs of parsley. Alternatively, serve in bowls over freshly cooked soba or noodles.

Note: This can be a warm or room-temperature dish. It can be prepared a few hours in advance, but it is best not to put the cooked chicken in the fridge because it will become tough. I always use spring chicken, as the meat is very tender.

Serves 4

SPICY CHICKEN WITH BASIL

Wonderful with a bowl of rice — comfort food at its best! To make it more children friendly you could reduce or omit the chilli bean sauce.

450g (1 lb) chicken thighs (skinless, boneless)
2 teaspoons light soya sauce
2 teaspoons Xiao Shing rice wine or dry sherry
1 teaspoon sesame oil
2 teaspoons cornflour
2 tablespoons oil
2 garlic cloves, peeled and coarsely chopped
2 teaspoons chilli bean sauce
2 teaspoons *hoisin* sauce
2 teaspoons oyster sauce
1 teaspoon dark soya sauce
1 teaspoon sugar
Large handful of fresh Thai basil leaves (rinsed and removed from stalk)

Cut the chicken into 2.5cm (1 inch) chunks and place in a bowl.

Combine the light soya sauce, Xiao Shing rice wine, sesame oil and cornflour with the chicken and mix to combine thoroughly.

Heat a wok or large non-stick frying pan with the oil until very hot and stir fry the chicken for five minutes or until slightly browned.

Add the rest of the ingredients except the basil and cook for an additional five minutes, stirring occasionally.

When the chicken is cooked, toss in the basil leaves and give the mixture a good stir. Serve at once with hot steamed rice.

Serves 2–4

EASY FISH STEW

One of our family favourites! It's simple and you can create your own combination.
Eat with some crusty bread and a dollop of *aioli*.

10–12 fresh tomatoes, or 2 cans of chopped peeled tomatoes
4 garlic cloves, peeled and chopped
½ onion, chopped
240ml (8 fl oz) dry white wine
Salt and pepper, to taste
12–16 mussels
180g (6 oz) fish fillet, such as cod or sea bass, cut into 2.5cm (1 inch) cubes
1–2 medium-sized squid hoods, cut into 1cm (½ inch) rings or 2 x 5cm (¾ x 2 inch) rectangles
that have been scored in diagonal slashes across the inside surface
8 scallops
8 medium-sized prawns, shelled and deveined
A sprinkle of saffron powder
2 tablespoons olive oil, divided

If using fresh tomatoes, soak them in hot water for five minutes then skin them and chop the flesh.

Heat one tablespoon olive oil in a deep frying pan and sauté the garlic and onion over a medium flame until softened. Add the chopped tomatoes and their juices and simmer until the sauce thickens. Add the white wine and simmer for 10 minutes.

Peel the prawns and set the meat aside. Place the heads and shells in a saucepan and add 480ml (16 fl oz) water. Bring to the boil then simmer until the liquid is reduced to 240ml (8 fl oz). Strain into a bowl and discard the solids. Add this shrimp stock to the tomato mixture and season lightly with salt and pepper. Take care not to add too much salt as the seafood itself is salty. The consistency of the tomato and prawn base should be like a thick soup; if necessary, reduce the liquid to thicken it.

Heat the tomato and seafood stock base. Heat one tablespoon of olive oil in a skillet and sauté the fish pieces and scallops slightly to sear them, then set them aside. When the tomato base is bubbling, add the squid followed by the fish and prawns. Add the mussels next. Cover the pan for a few minutes and cook until the mussel shells open, then stir in the scallops. Heat for another three minutes or so, then ladle into pasta bowls. Serve with hot French bread or garlic bread. Add a dollop of *aioli* over each serving of the stew, if you like.

Serves 6–8

STEAMED CLAMS WITH GARLIC AND CHILLI

The delicate amalgamation of clams, *sake*, garlic, orange and chilli is flawless!

1kg (2¼ lb) baby clams
80ml (2½ oz) vegetable oil
1 teaspoon sesame oil
6 garlic cloves, thinly sliced lengthways
2 small red chillies, seeded and thinly sliced
1 small leek, very thinly sliced
60ml (2 fl oz) drinking *sake*
Ground white pepper, to taste
1 teaspoon finely chopped ginger
A large pinch of *dashi* granules
15g (½ oz) butter
3 tablespoons chopped *mitsuba* or flat-leaf parsley
The juice of half an orange
Orange wedges, sliced between skin and flesh halfway through the wedge
240g (8 oz) vermicelli, freshly cooked
Coriander, to garnish
A pinch of salt

Soak the clams in several changes of cold water for about two hours to rid them of the sand. Drain well.

Heat the vegetable and sesame oils in a large saucepan over low heat, add the garlic and chilli, then cook, stirring often, until the garlic is golden brown but not burnt. Remove the garlic and chilli with a slotted spoon and drain on a paper towel.

Add the leeks to the pan and cook over low heat for five minutes, or until soft. Increase the heat then add the *sake*, clams, a pinch of salt, white pepper, ginger and the *dashi* granules. Cover and cook for five minutes, shaking the pan occasionally, until all the clams open. Discard any that are still closed. Stir in the garlic, chilli, butter, *mitsuba* or parsley and orange juice. Ladle into individual bowls over a small bed of hot vermicelli, adding a little liquid to each serving. Place a thin orange wedge on the side of each bowl and serve with a garnish of coriander.

Serves 4–6

TIAN OF PROVENÇAL VEGETABLES

A wonderful way of serving vegetables, either as a side dish or as the main course for a light lunch.

2 garlic cloves, crushed
125ml (4 fl oz) extra virgin olive oil
15g (½ oz) roughly chopped flat-leaf parsley
15g (½ oz) roughly chopped fresh basil
2 teaspoons fresh thyme
600g (20 oz), about 1 large aubergine, cut into 5mm thick slices
1 large potato, peeled and sliced into 2mm thick rounds
1 large zucchini, thinly into rounds about 2mm thick
4 ripe tomatoes, sliced about 5mm thick
80g (3 oz) *gruyère*, thinly sliced
Flat-leaf parsley
Sea salt and freshly ground black pepper, to taste

Preheat the grill to high.

Combine the crushed garlic, oil, flat-leaf parsley, thyme and basil in a bowl and season with sea salt and freshly ground black pepper.

Place the eggplant slices on an oven tray and brush generously with the herb mixture. Grill for five minutes or until golden.

Preheat the oven to 190°C (375°F).

In a shallow 28 x 32cm (11 x 14 inch) baking dish, arrange a layer of potatoes, slightly overlapping, then layer alternately with tomatoes, zucchini and eggplant, repeating the sequence to fill the dish. Tuck *gruyère* slices between the different vegetables and brush with three-quarters of the remaining herb mixture. Sprinkle with sea salt and freshly ground pepper. Bake the tian in the oven covered in foil for 25 minutes. Then bake it uncovered until the vegetables are tender and browned around the edges. Brush with the remaining herb mixture and serve hot or at room temperature, scattered with chopped flat-leaf parsley.

Serves 4–6

LAMB RACK IN MISO

Lamb is not commonly used in Japanese cooking but the *miso* is very subtle — it works amazingly well here!

2 x 8-rib racks of lamb
2 tablespoons white *miso*
2 tablespoons red *miso*
2 crushed garlic cloves
90g (3 oz) Japanese breadcrumbs
1 teaspoon finely chopped lemon zest
2 small handfuls *mitsuba* or flat-leaf parsley, finely chopped
60g (2 oz) butter, melted
Salt and pepper, to taste

Trim off the excess fat from around the bones of the lamb racks. Mix the white and red *miso* with the garlic. Rub the mixture over the lamb. Place in a dish and cover tightly with plastic wrap so the *miso* does not dry out. Refrigerate overnight.

When ready to cook, preheat the oven to 190°C (375°F).

To make the breadcrumb crust, combine the breadcrumbs, lemon zest, *mitsuba* (or parsley) and melted butter in a bowl. Season with a little salt and pepper.

Use a clean damp cloth to wipe the top bones of the racks to remove any *miso*, as it may burn — if you like, wrap the exposed bones with aluminium foil. Place the racks together so their bones interlock then stand them upright. This helps them to cook evenly.

Pat the breadcrumb mixture over the outside of the rack, pressing down so the crumbs adhere. Place the racks in a roasting tray and cook in the oven for about 35 minutes, or until done to your liking. Cut the lamb into cutlets and serve with some redcurrant jelly and mint sauce.

Serve with Pumpkin Mash and Sesame Spinach (recipes on pages 61 and 62).

Serves 6

PROVENÇAL BEEF DAUBE

Or simply, Beef Stew! This wonderful stew can be made in advance — don't be put off by the anchovies, you don't taste them but they add a depth to the sauce. Beef shin gives a wonderful soft meat, but any beef suitable for long cooking would do.

1 large celery stick
2 bay leaves
7 sprigs fresh thyme and parsley
4 juniper berries
1kg (2 lb 3 oz) lean braising beef, such as chuck, blade or beef shin
4 tablespoons olive oil, divided
225g (8 oz) thick-cut rindless streaky bacon or *pancetta*, cut into strips
2 onions, halved and thinly sliced
6 large garlic cloves, thinly sliced

½ bottle red wine
400ml (14 oz) beef stock, preferably home-made
350g (13 oz) carrots, cut into small chunky pieces
400g (14 oz) can chopped tomatoes
2 anchovies, rinsed and chopped [optional]
3 large strips pared orange zest
20g (¾ oz) softened butter
20g (¾ oz) plain (all-purpose) flour
100g (3½ oz) small black olives
Parsley for sprinkling
Salt and pepper, to taste

Preheat the oven to 150°C (300°F).

Make a *bouquet garni* by cutting the celery in half and sandwiching the bay leaves and herb sprigs in between. Tie everything into a tight bundle with some string.

Cut the meat into large chunks. Heat three tablespoons of the olive oil in a large casserole over a high heat. Brown the beef in batches until well coloured then season with salt and pepper. Add the bacon to the pan and fry until golden brown. Set aside with the beef.

Add the remaining oil and the onions to the casserole and fry for 10–12 minutes or until richly browned. Add the garlic and fry for an additional 1–2 minutes. Add the wine and simmer vigorously, scraping the bottom of the casserole to release the caramelized pieces, and simmer until the liquid has reduced by half.

Stir in the stock, return the beef and bacon to the casserole and add the carrots, tomatoes, anchovies, orange zest, *bouquet garni*, juniper berries and salt and pepper. Cover with foil and a tight-fitting lid and cook in the oven for two hours, or until the meat is meltingly tender.

Mash the butter and flour together to make a thickening paste (*beurre manié*). Remove the daube from the oven, uncover and skim off any excess oil. Discard the *bouquet garni* and orange zest and bring to a gentle simmer on the stove. Whisk in the *beurre manié* paste a little at a time until the sauce is thickened. Stir in the olives. Sprinkle with parsley and serve with pasta or mashed potato.

Serves 6–8

PASTA WITH CORN, BROCCOLINI, PEAS AND PARMESAN

Many people are trying to eat less meat. This pasta dish hits the spot in terms of taste, comfort and health!

4 ears of corn, husks and silks removed
1 bunch broccolini or broccoli, roughly chopped
50g (2 oz) peas, fresh or frozen
250g (9 oz) pasta (any type you wish)
100g (3½ oz) butter
1 red onion, finely chopped
2 garlic cloves, thinly sliced
30g (1 oz) grated parmesan or pecorino cheese, plus more to serve on the side
Sea salt and freshly ground pepper, to taste
60ml (2 fl oz) chicken stock or pasta water to moisten the sauce

Cut the kernels from the cob, place them in a saucepan with 375ml (13 oz) water and cook over medium heat for 8–10 minutes, or until tender. Process the corn and water in food processor or with a hand-held blender until roughly chopped. Set aside.

Bring a large saucepan of well-salted water to the boil. Cook the broccolini/broccoli and peas for two minutes or until tender but crisp. Remove with a slotted spoon and refresh in a bowl of ice water then drain. Cook the pasta in the same pan of water until *al dente*.

While the pasta is cooking, melt the butter in a large frying pan over medium heat and cook the onions and garlic for five minutes, or until soft. Season with sea salt and freshly ground pepper (be careful not to over season as the cheese is salty). Drain the pasta and add to the onions in the pan. Add the corn, peas and broccolini and toss until combined and heated through. If the sauce looks a little dry, add some hot chicken stock or pasta water to moisten. Add the cheese, then taste and adjust seasoning. Serve immediately with more cheese to scatter on individually.

Serves 4

GRILLED SPICED QUAIL

This is a simple recipe yet it never fails to impress and satisfy your palate! You can use the same marinade for pigeon or chicken, but quail just has that delicate texture and taste.

4 quails
1 teaspoon salt
1 juicy lemon
450g (15 oz) natural yoghurt
½ medium-sized onion, peeled and quartered
1 garlic clove, peeled
2cm (¾ inch) cube fresh ginger, peeled and quartered
½ fresh, hot green chilli, roughly sliced
2 teaspoons *garam masala*
(see right, or you may use ready-made mix)
Lime or lemon wedges

Garam masala
1 tablespoon black cardamom seeds
5cm (2 inch) piece of cinnamon stick
1 teaspoon black or regular cumin seeds
1 teaspoon cloves
1 teaspoon black peppercorns
¼ teaspoon nutmeg

Finely grind all *garam masala* ingredients together. Store in an airtight jar.

Cut the quail along both sides of the backbone to remove it. Open the body flat and remove all the bones except those in the legs and the wings. Sprinkle half the salt and squeeze the juice from ¾ of the lemon over the quails. Lightly rub the salt and lemon juice into the meat and skin. Set aside.

Combine the yoghurt, onion, garlic, ginger, green chilli and 2 teaspoons of *garam marsala* in a blender. Blend until the mixture becomes a smooth paste. Scrape the paste into a sieve set over a large bowl. Use a spatula to force the paste through the sieve. Discard the solids left in the sieve.

Put the quails in the marinade and mix well, making sure the marinade is rubbed thoroughly into the meat and skin. Cover and refrigerate for 6−24 hours.

When ready to cook, preheat the grill to high. Take the quails out of the marinade and shake off as much of it as possible. Arrange them skin-side up and cook under the grill for about 20 minutes, turning them over about halfway through and then once again towards the end, so the skin is browned nicely. Serve them hot with a squeeze of lime or lemon over a bed of thinly sliced lettuce, onions and tomatoes. The quails also go well with hot basmati or wild rice.

Serves 4

CHICKEN ADOBO — PHILIPPINE STYLE

Another simple dish that is tasty with a bowl of steaming rice and some stir-fried vegetables. A recipe from my wonderful cook Mel!

4 skinless chicken thighs
6 skinless drumsticks
12 garlic cloves, peeled and sliced
3 bay leaves
½ tablespoon whole black peppercorns
120ml (4 fl oz) white wine vinegar
90ml (3 fl oz) dark soya sauce
½ teaspoon sea salt
3 tablespoons sugar
½ teaspoon chicken powder
60ml (2 fl oz) water

In a large saucepan, stir together the garlic, bay leaves, peppercorns, vinegar, soya sauce, salt, sugar, chicken powder and water. Place the chicken in the saucepan and place over a medium-high heat. As soon as bubbles appear, lower the heat to a bare simmer and cover tightly. Turn the chicken pieces every 15–20 minutes so that they braise evenly. Continue to braise gently until the meat pulls easily away from the bone, 45–50 minutes in total.

If there is too much liquid, remove the chicken to a serving dish, bring the braising liquid to a boil and reduce until it reaches the consistency of thin syrup. Put the meat back into the sauce and taste — it should be quite sharp and lively. Turn the meat over to coat with the sauce and serve.

Options: You can also use a combination of chicken and pork, which is wonderful together. Use pork shoulder or even baby back ribs cut into individual pieces. Slightly fatty cuts are better as they tend not to dry out.

Note: If you can marinate the chicken in the ingredients for a few hours or even overnight, the flavours really are enhanced.

Serves 4

SPAGHETTI WITH ORIENTAL RAGU

A perfect fusion of East and West!

60ml (2 fl oz) vegetable oil, divided
1 teaspoon sesame oil, plus extra to drizzle
3 long tender aubergines, sliced 1.5cm (¾ inch) thick
3 garlic cloves, crushed
1½ teaspoons finely grated ginger
6 spring onions, sliced on the diagonal, white and green parts kept apart
600g (1 lb 4 oz) minced pork
1½ tablespoons chilli bean sauce
1½ tablespoons tomato paste
½ teaspoon *dashi* granules
2 tablespoons *mirin*
1 tablespoon Japanese soya sauce
1 teaspoon brown sugar
250g (9 oz) spaghetti, cooked

Put the sesame oil and half the vegetable oil in a wok over medium high heat. Add the aubergine pieces and stir-fry for about five minutes, or until golden on both sides. Drain on paper towels, squeeze out some of the oil and set aside.

Add the remaining vegetable oil to the wok then stir in the garlic, ginger and the white part of the spring onions. Cook for 30 seconds. Remove and set aside. Add the pork and use a spatula to break up the lumps. Brown the meat — this should take about six minutes.

Add the chilli bean sauce, tomato paste, *dashi* granules, *mirin*, soya sauce, sugar and 250ml (9 fl oz) water to the wok along with the spring onion and garlic mixture. Bring it to the boil then simmer for five minutes. Add the aubergine and most of the green part of the spring onion, reserving some for the garnish. Increase the heat to high and cook until most of the liquid has evaporated and the mixture has a slight glaze, about 4–5 minutes.

Serve with the freshly cooked spaghetti and sprinkle the reserved spring onion on top.

Serves 4

KOREAN BEEF

An all-time favourite for our boys!

240g (8 oz) *sukiyaki* beef

Marinade
3 garlic cloves, crushed
2 tablespoons sugar
1 tablespoon sesame oil
2 tablespoons Japanese soya sauce
2 tablespoons Japanese *sake*
A little salt and pepper
2 tablespoons oil

Mix the ingredients, except the oil, with the beef and marinate overnight.

Heat the oil in a skillet, add the beef and fry on high heat until it is lightly browned on both sides.

Serve immediately with rice, on a bed of salad or wrapped in lettuce leaves.

Serves 4

BACON-WRAPPED BAKED CHICKEN WITH SUN-DRIED TOMATOES

One of those tasty and easy-to-make dishes, with endless possibilities for the filling.

8 boneless skinless chicken thighs
8 slices of streaky bacon or *pancetta*
4 sprigs of rosemary
8 pieces sun-dried tomatoes in oil
60ml (2 fl oz) chicken stock
Salt and pepper, to taste

Preheat the oven to 190°C (375°F).

Slice open the chicken thighs and place a piece of sun-dried tomato in each. Close the thigh, wrap in bacon and secure with a toothpick. Place in an ovenproof dish and lay the rosemary on top. Bake for 30 minutes. Take dish out of the oven and discard the rosemary. Place the chicken on a baking sheet and bake in the oven until the bacon becomes crispy, approximately 4–5 minutes on each side.

In the meantime, pour off some of the fat from the baking dish and de-glaze the dish with a little chicken stock. Boil and reduce by half. Season with salt and pepper to taste.

Serve the chicken with the sauce drizzled on top.

Option: Add goat cheese to the sun-dried tomato stuffing.

Serves 4

ASIAN-STYLE BARBECUED SPARE RIBS

A true boat or picnic favourite. Asian-inspired and a true crowd pleaser, young and old.

2 racks baby pork ribs, about 1.8kg (4 lbs), cut into individual ribs
60ml (¼ cup) *hoisin* sauce
60ml (¼ cup) dark soya sauce
3 tablespoons runny honey
2 tablespoons ginger juice (grate a piece of fresh peeled ginger then squeeze out the juice)

Mix all the ingredients in a bowl.

Place the ribs in a large plastic zip-lock bag and pour in the marinade. Seal the bag and press out any excess air. Marinate the ribs in the fridge for 24 hours, turning the bag occasionally.

Preheat the oven to 180°C (350°F).

Transfer the ribs and marinade to a roasting pan large enough to hold them in one layer. Roast the ribs, turning them every 30 minutes, until they are tender and well browned.

Serves 6

LAMB LOIN WITH ORANGE AND MINT CRUST

I got the idea for this dish from a complicated traditional English recipe from Sussex. I simplified it, as I like the combination of orange and mint.

1.5kg (3 lb 2 oz) lamb loin fillets, cut into 6–8 pieces
6 tablespoons dry breadcrumbs
30 g (1 oz) butter
1 tablespoon chopped parsley
1¼ tablespoons chopped chives
½ tablespoon chopped mint leaves
2 teaspoons grated orange zest
2 tablespoons orange juice
1 egg, beaten
Salt and pepper, to taste
2 tablespoons oil, for pan frying

Sauce
280ml (10 fl oz) lamb or veal stock
60g (2 oz) butter
1 teaspoon flour
1 tablespoon redcurrant jelly
1 tablespoon orange juice
60ml (2 fl oz) Cointreau

Season the loin pieces with salt and pepper and set aside.

Mix the butter, parsley, chives, mint, orange juice and zest, egg and salt and pepper together and rub thoroughly over the meat. Roll the loin in the breadcrumbs until it is covered evenly. Set aside.

Heat the lamb or veal stock until simmering then keep it hot. Melt the 60g of butter in a saucepan and heat slowly until it becomes nutty-brown in colour. Mix in the flour and stir well until it becomes a smooth paste. Add the Cointreau, boil until reduced by half then stir into the stock. Add the redcurrant jelly, orange juice and salt and pepper to taste.

Heat two tablespoons of oil in a non-stick pan over medium heat. Panfry the loin evenly on all sides until the meat is cooked to your liking. Slice and serve with the redcurrant sauce.

Note: You can substitute with other red meats, such as beef, veal, pork or even venison.

Serves 4–6

PROVENÇAL FISH FILLETS

A typical way of serving fish in the south of France. What better combination could there be than fish, sweet tomatoes, olives — and of course, the sun!

225g (8 oz) small shallots or small white baby onions, unpeeled
50g (2 oz) butter
1 teaspoon sugar
320g (11 oz) young leeks, finely sliced on the diagonal
4 skinned fish fillets, 125g (4 oz) each, such as sole or plaice
100ml (4 fl oz) olive oil
100ml (4 fl oz) dry white wine
300ml (10 fl oz) fish stock
200g (7 oz) cherry tomatoes, halved or quartered
75g (3 oz) pitted black olives
Flat leaf parsley and lemon halves, to garnish
Salt and pepper, to taste

Place the shallots in a pan of water, bring to the boil and cook for five minutes. Drain and plunge into a bowl of cold water. Trim the ends, peel off the skins and dry well.

Heat half the butter in a frying pan, add the shallots and sugar and cook over low heat for five minutes or until golden. Add the leeks and cook for 4–5 minutes until just tender. Set aside.

Season the fish with salt and pepper. Heat the olive oil and remaining butter in a frying pan. Fry the fish for about three minutes on each side. Remove from the pan and keep warm.

Pour the wine into the pan, bring to the boil and simmer until reduced by half. Add the stock, return to the boil and cook for 10 minutes or until syrupy. Add the tomatoes and the olives and simmer for one minute. Return the shallots and leeks to the pan to warm through. Season to taste and spoon over the fish. Garnish and serve.

Serves 4

VEGETABLE TRIO

PUMPKIN MASH
This is always such a hit with all our friends, and a truly healthy alternative to the traditional mash.

1.8kg (4 lbs) Japanese pumpkin,
seeded and cut into 4–5 equal pieces
Vegetable oil
Sea salt, to taste
120g (4 oz) butter, diced

¼ teaspoon sesame oil
2 teaspoons Japanese soya sauce
1½ teaspoons finely grated ginger and juice
White pepper, to taste

Preheat the oven to 200°C (400°F). Place the pumpkin pieces skin-side down in a roasting tray, drizzle with vegetable oil and sprinkle with sea salt. Roast for about 1½ hours, or until tender. Scoop the flesh from the skin and put in a bowl. Add the butter and sesame oil. Mash until it is very smooth, stir in the soya sauce, ginger and juice, then season with a little salt and pepper to taste. Reheat gently, if needed.

BEETROOT AND BROCCOLI SALAD
A colourful and delectable salad that will complement almost any dish!

1 head of broccoli, cut into florets
6 pieces fresh baby corn
¼ yellow pepper (capsicum), sliced lengthways
1 medium-sized cooked beetroot,
sliced 5mm (¼ inch) thick
60g (2 oz) shredded carrots

3–4 tablespoons extra virgin olive oil
3–4 teaspoons white wine vinegar
2 anchovy fillets, mashed
½ an orange, cut into segments
without the membranes, skin and pith
Salt and pepper, to taste

Boil the broccoli in salted water until just cooked. Drain and set aside to cool. Whisk together the olive oil, wine vinegar, anchovies, salt and pepper in salad bowl. Add the remaining ingredients and you have a tasty salad with a lovely mix of textures and colours.

VEGETABLE TRIO, cont'd

SESAME SPINACH
A simple and easy-to-prepare side dish.

600g (20 oz) spinach
2 tablespoons oil
1 teaspoon salt

Sauce
3 tablespoons sesame paste
6 tablespoons warm water
1 tablespoon white vinegar
2 teaspoons soya sauce
1 tablespoon brown sugar

Wash the spinach and boil in a large pot of water with the oil and salt. When the spinach is tender, drain it and let cool.

Mix all the sauce ingredients together.

Squeeze as much liquid as possible from the spinach then align the leaves on a chopping board. Cut them into 5cm (2 inch) long sections and make little bundles of a few sections of spinach tied with a spinach stem. To serve, spoon a little of the sauce over each bundle. This can be prepared hours in advance and sauced just before serving.

Serves 4–6

MELT-IN-YOUR-MOUTH VEAL MEATBALLS

A recipe given to me by a wonderful friend, Laurence, after she served it to me one jet-lagged night in Paris. The best meatballs I have tasted!

500g (18 oz) minced veal
1 onion, finely chopped
50g (2 oz) dry breadcrumbs
4 large eggs
50g (2 oz) grated Emmenthal (Swiss) cheese
50g (2 oz) grated parmesan cheese
2 tablespoons olive oil, plus more for frying
1 large handful of flat leafed parsley, chopped
Salt and pepper, to taste
Olive oil, for pan frying

Fresh tomato sauce
600g (1 lb 5oz) Roma (plum) or vine tomatoes, roughly chopped
10g (¼ oz) unsalted butter
1 tablespoon olive oil
1 tablespoon sugar (adjust depending on how sweet the tomatoes are)
1 tablespoon tomato paste (again adjust depending on how flavourful the tomatoes are)
salt and milled black pepper

Gently mix all the ingredients in a bowl until well blended. The mixture should be moist. Season, but be careful with the salt as the cheeses are quite salty.

Heat a large non-stick frying pan with olive oil.

Form small flattened meatballs about the size of golf balls. Fry until golden and crisp on each side.

Serve with a fresh tomato sauce and pasta or rice.

Fresh tomato sauce
Heat the butter and olive oil in a frying pan. When hot, add the tomatoes, sugar, tomato paste, salt and pepper. Cook until the liquid has evaporated and you have a rich tomato sauce.

Serves 6–8

ROAST PIGEON

One of my favourite dishes at my parents' house, where my siblings and I call it *'Bo Bo Ho'*, meaning every bowl/meal is amazing! One just cannot believe how simple it is.

1 pigeon

Marinade
1 tablespoon *chu hau* sauce
1 tablespoon preserved red beancurd
1 tablespoon sugar
1 tablespoon Xiao Shing rice wine

Mix the marinade ingredients together and rub thoroughly over the pigeon, especially under the legs and the wings. Leave for at least three hours or overnight.

Preheat the oven to 180°C (350°F).

Roast for about 40 minutes, or until the skin is golden and crisp. To serve the Chinese way, chop the pigeon into small, even pieces. You can also serve it halved on a plate with rice, or shred it and arrange over a bed of salad.

Note: Chu hau sauce is a thick dark brown seasoning paste made from beans, flour and spices. It is commonly used in Chinese stews and braised dishes. You can find it in most stores that sell Chinese sauces and spices.

Serves 2

ROASTED VEGETABLE AND PASTA GRATIN

A non-meat dish, but equally loved by non-vegetarians!

400g (1 lb) aubergines (eggplant)
700g (1 lb 8 oz) mixed peppers [optional — my family *hates* any type of pepper!]
450g (1 lb) squash, e.g. butternut or pumpkin, peeled
125g (4½ oz) cherry tomatoes
90ml (3 oz) olive oil
225g (8 oz) dried pasta shapes such as penne or fusilli
450g (1 lb) frozen leaf spinach, thawed
225g (8 oz) mature Cheddar or *gruyère* cheese
50g (2 oz) unsalted butter
50g (2 oz) flour
900ml (32 oz) milk
30ml (1 oz) wholegrain mustard
150g (5 oz) soft cheese with garlic and herbs such as Boursin
Salt and pepper, to taste

Preheat the oven to 220°C (425°F).

Cut the aubergines, mixed peppers and squash into bite-sized pieces and put into roasting tins and mix with the cherry tomatoes and oil. Roast for 45 minutes or until tender and slightly charred. Reduce the heat to 200°C (400°F).

Cook the pasta in boiling salted water until *al dente* and drain thoroughly. Squeeze the excess liquid from the frozen spinach. Grate the cheese.

Melt the butter in a pan then stir in the flour. Cook, stirring constantly, for one minute before adding the milk. Simmer for 2–3 minutes or until the sauce thickens. Remove from the heat and add the mustard, soft cheese and all but 50g (1½ oz) of the Cheddar or *gruyère*. Stir thoroughly until smooth and season with salt and pepper.

Mix the pasta, spinach and roasted vegetables and sauce in a large, shallow, ovenproof dish and sprinkle the remaining 50g (1½ oz) Cheddar cheese over the top.

Place the dish on a baking sheet and cook at 200°C (400°F) for about 40 minutes or until golden.

Serves 8

CALAMARI 'ARANCIA' (ORANGE-GLAZED SQUID)

A great dish to serve with drinks or as a starter. The delicate orange flavour mingling with the fresh squid makes this dish very special.

720g (1½ lb) squid hoods, cleaned
3 garlic cloves, crushed
1 teaspoon ground sweet paprika
2 teaspoons grated orange zest
1 tablespoon orange juice
1 tablespoon red wine vinegar
60g (2 oz) brown sugar
1 tablespoon olive oil
1 tablespoon chopped fresh coriander
Oil, for the pan

Cut the squid open and score the inner surface with shallow diagonal slashes, before cutting it into 2 x 5cm (¾ x 2 inch) pieces.

Combine the squid, garlic, paprika, orange zest and juice, vinegar, sugar and olive oil in medium bowl. Cover and refrigerate for at least three hours or overnight.

Drain the squid over a bowl and reserve the marinade.

Cook the squid in hot, oiled griddle pan, or (even better) under the grill or on the barbecue. Cook it in batches until the pieces start to curl and are almost cooked. Pour the reserved marinade into a pan and simmer, uncovered, for about one minute or until slightly thickened.

Combine the squid, marinade and coriander in bowl and serve, either as an *hors d'oeuvre* over a bed of salad leaves, or as a starter over a bowl of freshly cooked pasta.

Serves 6–8

OMA'S ROAST PORK

This is my Austrian grandmother's way of cooking roast pork. She was the most amazing cook.

1½ kg (3 lb) pork shoulder or loin (I prefer shoulder or bone-in loin as they have more flavour)
1 tablespoon caraway seeds
1 teaspoon dried marjoram
1 tablespoon sea salt, or to taste
2 garlic cloves, pressed
2–3 tablespoons butter
2 medium onions, peeled and quartered
Chicken stock
1 heaped tablespoon sour cream
Salt and pepper, to taste

Preheat the oven to 200°C (400°F).

Chop the salt, marjoram and caraway seeds on a chopping board, then add the garlic and butter. Rub the mixture thoroughly into the pork. Place the pork in a roasting pan and cook for 15 minutes and then lower the heat to 180°C.

After 15 minutes, add 60ml boiling water to roasting pan. Every 20 mins or so, keep adding boiling water to the pan to ensure bottom of the pan does not dry out. Occasionally use the pan juices to also baste the meat. Continue roasting for approximately 1½ to 2 hours until a thermometer inserted diagonally at least 5cm (2 inch) into the meat registers 150°C (300°F). During the last half hour add the onions to the pan and baste with the pan juices. Do not add them earlier as they will burn and make the sauce bitter.

When the pork is cooled, transfer the meat to a cutting board and cover loosely with foil. Leave it to stand for 10 minutes while making the sauce.

Make the sauce by deglazing the roasting pan with a little chicken stock. Reduce the pan juices slightly. Adjust seasoning to taste with salt and pepper and add one heaped tablespoon of sour cream.

Slice the pork and serve with the sauce.

Serves 4–6

KIN'S BEEF SATAY, SATAY SAUCE AND SHRIMP SAMBAL CONDIMENT

The satay is another of my mum's great recipes! The satay sauce is simply one of the best. Once you have made this yourself, satay elsewhere is never quite the same.

BEEF SATAY
960g (2 lbs) of beef fillet

To serve: cubes of raw cucumber, raw onion and rice cakes

Seasoning
6 small shallots
3 garlic cloves
3 candlenuts (found in Malay or Thai grocery stores)
¾ teaspoon chopped or grated fresh ginger

Marinade
½ tablespoon coriander powder
1 teaspoon cumin powder
1 teaspoon fennel powder
1 teaspoon ground pepper
½ teaspoon ground nutmeg
1 teaspoon salt
4 tablespoons sugar
1 tablespoons dark soya sauce
1½ tablespoons light soya sauce
30ml (1 fl oz) *assam* water,
made by soaking a 5mm (¼ inch) cube of tamarind paste in 30ml (1 fl oz) hot water
1 teaspoon chicken powder

Remove the gristle from the meat, slice it into two layers lengthwise, then cut at a slant into pieces of about 1cm (½ inch) thick and 7.5cm (3 inch) wide. Pound the beef with the back of a knife, then cut it into 2.5cm (1 inch) square pieces.

Blend the seasoning ingredients into a paste. Combine into the marinade, then add the beef. Mix well and marinate in the fridge for at least 12 hours.

Thread the meat onto bamboo skewers. Brush the meat with oil before grilling or cooking on the barbecue.

KIN'S BEEF SATAY, SATAY SAUCE
AND SHRIMP SAMBAL CONDIMENT, cont'd

SATAY SAUCE

4 teaspoons oil
5 small shallots
3 garlic cloves
3 red chillies (more if you like it hot)
5mm (¼ inch) piece of *blanchan* (shrimp paste)
1 stalk of lemongrass
1cm (½ inch) piece of Thai ginger (*lengkua or galangal*)
½ teaspoon chilli powder

240ml (8 fl oz) of coconut milk
30ml (1 fl oz) *assam* water
240ml (8 fl oz) chicken stock
or water with chicken powder
5 tablespoons sugar
½ teaspoon salt
½ teaspoon chicken powder
480–600 grams (1–1¼ lbs) skinned roasted peanuts

Finely grind the shallots, garlic, chillies, *blanchan*, lemongrass, Thai ginger and chilli powder. Heat 4 teaspoons of oil in pan. Sauté the finely ground ingredients for 10 minutes, until it smells fragrant. Add the *assam* water and coconut milk. Bring to the boil then add the peanuts. Keep stirring until you see the oil floating to the surface. Add the chicken stock or water. Bring to the boil, add the sugar and salt and adjust seasonings to taste.

Serves 6

MALAYSIAN SHRIMP SAMBAL
A great condiment to go with noodles, congee, etc. Homemade is the best! This family recipe is from my sister-in-law's father, Uncle Cheuk Man, who lives in Kuala Lumpur.

1 cup garlic cloves, peeled
1 cup shallots, peeled
420g (14 oz) dried shrimp, soaked for 10 minutes then drained
5–6 small hot red chillies, or to taste
6mm square (¼ inch square) *blanchan* (shrimp paste)
3 tablespoons oil

Blend the above ingredients to a paste then cook slowly in the oil for up to four hours, or until dry. Stir frequently, and add a little more oil if it starts to stick to the pan. Let it cool before storing in an airtight container in a cool place.

Make sure you open all the windows in the kitchen and close the kitchen door while cooking this sambal — the aroma does linger.

Serve over noodles or with salad for the authentic Malaysian kick!

VEAL WITH ZUCCHINI AND BASIL

A great all-in-one dish. Great for dinner parties as almost all of it can be prepared in advance.

1.5kg (3 lb 5 oz) veal shoulder, deboned
120g (4 oz) butter
2 onions, finely chopped
20g (¾ oz) flour
750ml (26 fl oz) chicken stock
1 *bouquet garni* (you can buy this in a delicatessen or make your own by adding 3 sprigs of thyme
and parsley and 2 bay leaves to the casserole)
1 bunch basil
500g (17 oz) carrots, peeled, halved and quartered lengthwise and cut into 5cm (2 inch) pieces
50g (2 oz) pearl onions
500g (17 oz) zucchini, halved and quartered and cut into 5cm (2 inch) pieces
3 tablespoons sugar
750ml (26 fl oz) whipping cream
Salt and pepper, to taste
Fresh basil, to garnish

Cut the veal into 3cm (1¼ inch) cubes. In a large casserole, melt half the butter, add the meat in batches and brown well. Add the onions and cook slowly for five minutes. Dust with the flour and cook until it starts to brown then stir in the chicken stock. Add the *bouquet garni*, basil and salt and pepper. Cover and cook on a low fire, 45 minutes to 1 hour.

While the meat is cooking, prepare the vegetables separately. Put the carrots in a pan with enough water to cover them halfway and add 20g (¾ oz) butter and one tablespoon sugar. Bring to a boil and cook until the water evaporates and the carrots are still slightly crisp. Place in a warm serving dish. Cook the onions and zucchini in the same way.

When the veal is tender, lift the meat out of the sauce with a slotted spoon and keep it warm. Pour the sauce through a sieve and discard the solids. Return the sauce to the casserole pan and boil to reduce by half. Add the cream and reduce again. Taste and adjust the seasoning.

Reheat the vegetables and mix with the meat. Pour the sauce over the meat and vegetables and garnish with plenty of chopped fresh basil.

Serves 6

GOOD OL' BARBARA'S KEDGEREE

A slight variation of the Indian/British dish passed down from Barbara, my mother-in-law. It can be a side dish, a light main dish or even breakfast!

1 tablespoon vegetable oil
1 garlic clove, chopped
1 small onion, chopped
½ teaspoon saffron powder
½ teaspoon curry powder

480g (16 oz) long-grain rice, cooked and cooled
2–4 fillets of smoked trout, together 150–200g (5–7 oz), or more for a substantial main dish, grilled, skinned and flaked into small chunks
(you may use other types of fish, such as smoked haddock or salmon)
1–2 tablespoons fish stock or water
2 hard-boiled eggs, chopped
60g (2 oz) sultanas, or more
A sprinkle of Maggi sauce
3–4 shallots, peeled, sliced finely and deep fried
Croutons
Salt and pepper, to taste

Sauté the garlic in oil for one minute, then add the onion and sauté until soft. Add the saffron and curry powder, mix well and fry until fragrant. Add the rice and stir well.

Thoroughly mix in the trout and fold in evenly over a medium flame until the mixture is heated through. Add 1–2 tablespoons of the fish stock or water then mix in the chopped egg and the sultanas. Season with salt and black pepper. Spoon immediately onto serving plates, sprinkle with a few drops of Maggi sauce and add the fried shallots and croutons on top.

Serves 2–4

COD WITH A FENNEL AND SAFFRON SAUCE

An elegant and delicate dish.

4 cod fillets, 200g (7 oz) each
8 tablespoon butter, divided
8 saffron strands
1 leek, trimmed and finely sliced
1 fennel bulb, thinly sliced, sprigs retained
120ml (4 fl oz) white wine
180ml (6 fl oz) fish or chicken stock
1 teaspoon sugar
Sea salt, to taste

Rinse the fillets and pat them dry with a paper towel. Lightly season with sea salt; set aside.

Melt 4 tablespoons butter in a large heavy-based frying pan over medium heat and cook the saffron for one minute or until dark. Add the leek and fennel slices and cook for 2–3 minutes, or until the leek is soft. Stir in the wine and sugar and boil until reduced by half.

Melt the remaining butter in another frying pan over medium heat and fry the cod fillets on each side to brown. Add the fillets to the leek and fennel mixture, cover and simmer for about three minutes, or until the fish is done.

Divide the fillets between four warmed plates then spoon sauce over the top. Garnish with the reserved fennel tops and serve with boiled new potatoes and a green salad.

Serves 4

CANTONESE STEAM MINCED PORK

A stay-at-home, family-style Cantonese dish!

480g (1 lb) of semi-fatty pork (*mui tao* cut), finely minced by hard chopping

Marinade
1 egg white
1½ teaspoons chicken powder
1½ tablespoons Xiao Shing rice wine
1½ teaspoons light soya sauce
1½ tablespoons oyster sauce
1½ tablespoons sugar
1 teaspoon ginger juice
1 teaspoon sesame oil
1 tablespoon cornflour
¼ cup water

Use chopsticks or a fork to thoroughly mix all the marinade ingredients except the cornflour and water into the pork. Add the cornflour then stir in the water a little at a time. Refrigerate for at least three hours or even overnight.

When ready to cook, put the mixture in a shallow dish with a little room to spare as the liquid will be released from the pork, making the *jus*. Steam over simmering water for 40 minutes. This is traditionally served straight from the steaming dish but it can be made in individual portions.

There are many alternatives to the dish, for example:

Top with slivers of salted fish and steam
Top with chopped, boiled salted duck eggs
You can also pan-fry the individual patties!

Serves 4–6

TASTY BEEF WITH GARLIC AND SWEET SOYA SAUCE

An Asian-inspired dish — a delicious mixture of sweet and salty.

500g (1 lb 2 oz) beef tenderloin
1 teaspoon sesame oil
60ml (2 fl oz) white vinegar
6 garlic cloves, peeled and finely chopped
1 teaspoon salt
1 teaspoon pepper
1½ teaspoon sugar
4 tablespoons sweet soya sauce (*kecap manis*)
4 shallots
½ tablespoon sesame seeds
500 ml (16½ fl oz) oil, for deep frying

Cut the beef tenderloin into 5cm (¼ inch) long strips.

Marinate the beef, preferably overnight, with salt, pepper, sesame oil, vinegar, chopped garlic and sugar.

Peel the shallots and slice them finely. Fry in oil until crisp then drain and set aside.

Heat 2 cups of oil in a large heavy-based pan or wok. When it's hot, add the beef with the marinade. Fry until the marinade starts to caramelize in the oil and the beef begins to crisp. Add the sweet soya sauce, shallots and sesame seeds and stir through.

Place a sieve over a large bowl and pour the beef mixture into the sieve to drain the oil.

Serve with rice or, alternatively, in lettuce cups as an appetizer.

Serves 6–8

SLOW-BRAISED LAMB SHANKS IN A RED WINE SAUCE

An exceptionally easy recipe that produces a meat so tender it literally melts in the mouth. Kids love it.

6 lamb shanks, trimmed
2 tablespoons olive oil
460ml (16 fl oz) chicken or beef stock
240ml (8 fl oz) red wine
6 bay leaves
4 garlic cloves, peeled and halved
12 baby onions, peeled
1 large sprig rosemary
2 large sprigs thyme
3 sprigs marjoram or 1 teaspoon dried
1 tablespoon black peppercorns
1 tablespoon redcurrant or cranberry jam
Salt, to taste

Preheat the oven to 160°C (320°F).

Place a frying pan over high heat with the olive oil. Add the lamb shanks to the pan and brown thoroughly on all sides. This may have to be done in batches.

Place the lamb in a baking dish with the stock, wine, bay leaves, garlic, onion, herbs and peppercorns. Season with salt. Cover the dish with foil and bake for two hours, or until the lamb is very tender. Remove the foil for the last 20 minutes to let the shanks brown slightly.

Remove the shanks from baking dish, cover and set aside.

To make the sauce spoon off some of the fat in the baking dish and scrape down the sides of the pan to get all the brown bits. Add the redcurrant or cranberry jam and stir thoroughly. Mash one or two of the (by now) very soft garlic cloves into the sauce. Remove the herbs with a slotted spoon. Taste the sauce and adjust the seasonings, if necessary.

Serve the lamb shanks with mashed potatoes and plenty of the sauce.

Serves 6

SWEET

"Baking is a precise art — follow directions. Cooking is a free art — follow your heart!"

Claudia

CARAMELIZED BANANA TARTLETS

This is for those who hate rolling out pastry — the crust gets pressed into the pan rather than rolled out.

Crust
120g (4 oz) unsalted butter, room temperature
60g (2 oz) icing (powdered) sugar
90g (3 oz) almonds, lightly toasted,
then finely ground (with skin)
1 teaspoon finely grated orange zest
½ teaspoon vanilla extract
¼ teaspoon salt
125g (4½ oz) plain (all-purpose) flour

Filling
4 tablespoons unsalted butter, divided
6 large bananas, slightly under-ripe, peeled and
cut on the diagonal into 1cm (½ inch) slices
100g (3½ oz) sugar, divided
Juice of 1 lemon
4 tablespoons warm water

Preheat the oven to 180°C (350°F).

Use a food processor to beat the first six ingredients to combine. Add the flour and mix until moist clumps form. Gather the dough into a ball and flatten into a disc. Wrap in plastic and chill for 30 minutes.

Divide the dough into six equal pieces. Press each piece evenly onto the bottom and up the sides of an 11cm (4½ inch) tartlet pan with a removable bottom. Bake the crusts until deep brown and cooked through, about 25 minutes. Cool on a rack.

For the filling, melt two tablespoons of butter in a large non-stick pan over medium heat until it starts to brown. Add half the bananas to the pan in a single layer and cook until brown on the bottom. Use a thin spatula to turn the slices over then sprinkle 30g (¼ cup) of sugar evenly over the bananas. Cook occasionally, swirling the pan, until the sugar dissolves and turns golden, about three minutes. Turn the banana slices over; add two tablespoons of warm water and half the lemon juice: continue cooking, occasionally swirling the pan, until the caramel thickens slightly, about two minutes. Arrange the banana slices in three of the tartlets crusts; spoon any caramel from the pan over the filling.

Repeat the process with remaining ingredients.

Makes 6 tartlets

PASSION FRUIT PARFAIT

A simple yet satisfying light summer dessert.

6 egg rings

Parfait
3 teaspoons gelatine powder
2 tablespoons water
About 180g (6 oz) pulp from 4 passion fruit
120g (4 fl oz) double cream
60g (2 oz) caster sugar
1 tablespoon lemon juice

Mango coulis
1 ripe medium-sized mango, peeled flesh removed by cutting on both sides of the flat stone, then diced
60g (2 oz) caster sugar
60ml (2 fl oz) water
1 tablespoon lemon juice

Sprinkle the gelatine powder over the water and let it dissolve. Melt the gelatine by placing it over a pan of hot water, then let it cool slightly.

Mix the passion fruit pulp, cream, sugar and lemon juice in a bowl. Stir the gelatine into the passion fruit mixture. Lightly oil 6 egg rings and place them on serving plates. Pour the passion fruit mixture into the egg rings and refrigerate for several hours, or until set.

To make the mango coulis, mix together the diced mango, sugar and water and bring to a boil. Reduce the heat and simmer uncovered for two minutes. Cool the mixture, then blend until smooth then add the lemon juice.

When ready to serve, remove the rings from the parfaits. Decorate with some sliced fruit and serve with a small pool of coulis around the parfait.

Serves 6

ULTIMATE CARAMEL BROWNIES

A rich alternative to the standard brownie.

Brownies
120g (4 oz) unsalted butter
180g (6 oz) bittersweet chocolate
(or dark 60% cacao) chopped
100g (3½ oz) plain (all-purpose) flour
½ teaspoon baking powder
2 large eggs
200g (7 oz) sugar
¼ teaspoon table salt
2 teaspoons vanilla extract
60g (2 oz) chopped pecans
60g (2 oz) semisweet or white chocolate chips

Caramel
60ml (2 fl oz) plus 1 tablespoon heavy cream
¼ teaspoon table salt
60ml (2 fl oz) water
2 tablespoons light corn syrup
250g (9 oz) sugar
2 tablespoons unsalted butter
1 teaspoon vanilla extract

For the caramel, combine the cream and salt in a small bowl and stir well to dissolve. Combine the water and corn syrup in a heavy-bottomed 2–3 quart saucepan. Pour the sugar into the centre of the saucepan, taking care not to let the sugar granules touch the sides of the pan.

Gently stir with a clean spatula to moisten the sugar thoroughly. Cover and bring to a boil over medium-high heat; cook, covered and without stirring, until the sugar is completely dissolved and the liquid is clear, 3–5 minutes. Uncover and continue to cook without stirring until the bubbles show a faint golden colour, 3–5 minutes more. Reduce the heat to medium-low. Continue to cook (swirling occasionally) until the caramel is light amber and registers about 185°C (365°F) on a candy or instant-read thermometer, 1–3 minutes longer. Remove the saucepan from the heat and carefully add the cream to the centre of pan. Stir with a whisk or spatula (the mixture will bubble and steam vigorously) until the cream is fully incorporated and the bubbling subsides.

Stir in the butter and vanilla until combined then transfer the caramel to a microwaveable measuring cup or bowl and set aside.

For the brownies, adjust the oven rack to the lower-middle position; heat oven to 160°C (320°F). Lightly spray 22cm (9 inch) square baking pan with non-stick cooking spray.

ULTIMATE CARAMEL BROWNIES, cont'd

Melt the butter and bittersweet chocolate in a medium heatproof bowl set over a saucepan of barely simmering water, stirring occasionally, until smooth and combined; set aside to cool slightly. Alternatively melt the butter and chocolate in a microwave on a low setting. Whisk together the flour and baking powder in a small bowl; set aside. Whisk the eggs in a large bowl, add the sugar, salt and vanilla and whisk until incorporated. Add the melted chocolate and butter to the egg mixture and whisk until homogeneous. Add the flour and stir with a rubber spatula until almost combined. Add the chopped pecans and chocolate chips (if using); mix until incorporated and no flour streaks remain.

Evenly spread half the brownie batter into the prepared baking pan. Drizzle a scant 60ml (¼ cup) of caramel over the batter. Drop the remaining batter in large mounds over the caramel layer and spread evenly into the pan with a rubber spatula. Drizzle an additional scant 60ml (¼ cup) caramel over the top. Using the tip of a butter knife, swirl the caramel and batter. Bake the brownies until a toothpick inserted into the centre comes out with only a few moist crumbs attached, 35 to 40 minutes. Place the pan on a wire rack and let the brownies cool to room temperature, about 1½ hours.

Heat the remaining caramel (you should have about 180ml or ¾ cup) for 45–60 seconds in the microwave until warm and pourable but still thick (do not boil), stirring once or twice. Pour the caramel over the brownies. Use a spatula to spread the caramel evenly over the surface. Refrigerate the brownies, uncovered, for at least two hours.

Use a chef's knife to cut the brownies into 25 evenly sized squares. Press a pecan half onto the surface of each piece. Serve chilled or at room temperature.

Makes 25 squares

MANGO TARTE TATIN

A classic tartlet but with the exotic taste of mangoes!

1kg (2 lb) apples, peeled, cored and diced
45g (1½ oz) unsalted butter, plus extra for the moulds
45g (1½ oz) apricot jam
4 ripe medium-sized mangoes, peeled and halved,
the flesh removed by cutting on both sides of the flat stone
240g (8 oz) caster sugar
150g (5 oz) unsalted butter, diced into small pieces
2 tablespoons desiccated coconut, for decoration

1kg (2 lb) puff pastry

Preheat the oven to 200ºC (400ºF).

Put the apples and butter in a saucepan, cover and cook until soft. Stir in the apricot jam and mix well. Set aside.

Butter eight 7.5–10cm (3–4 inch) tartlet moulds and coat them with sugar. Put a mango half in the bottom of each mould, round side down, then cover with the apple compote.

On a lightly floured board, roll out the pastry to 3mm (⅛ inch) thick and cut out rounds about 1.25cm (½ inch) larger than the tops of the moulds. Cover each mould with a pastry round, gently pushing the overhang into the inside of the mould. Place the moulds on a tray and bake the tartlets for 25 minutes or until done.

Make the caramel sauce. Heat the sugar in a heavy-based saucepan until it melts and turns golden nutty brown. Remove from the heat and whisk in the butter.

When the tartlets are baked, turn them onto plates with the pastry side down. Drizzle some caramel over them and serve immediately with a scoop of vanilla ice-cream.

Serves 8

PEAR HONEY CAKE

This can also be made with Golden Delicious or other tart apples.

60g (2 oz) salted butter
300g (9 oz) sugar, divided
4 firm-ripe pears, cored and thinly sliced
375g (14 oz) plain (all-purpose) flour
2 teaspoons baking powder
¼ teaspoon salt
Zest and juice of 1 lemon
240g (8 oz) unsalted butter at room temperature
2 large eggs
5 tablespoons honey
2 teaspoons pure vanilla extract
120ml (4 fl oz) milk

Preheat the oven to 160°C (320°F).

Combine the salted butter and 100g (3 oz) of the sugar in a large non-stick saucepan over medium heat. Stir until the sugar bubbles begin to caramelize. Add the pear slices a few at a time, cooking for about five minutes, or just until they begin to soften and brown. Add the lemon juice. Transfer to a plate and set aside.

Grease a 30cm (12 inch) cake tin. Sift together the flour, baking powder and salt. Beat the unsalted butter and the remaining 200g (6 oz) sugar until light and fluffy. Add the lemon zest. Beat in the eggs and honey until blended. Mix together the vanilla and milk. With the mixer on low speed, add the flour mixture, alternating with the milk and mixing just until the dry ingredients are moist. Do not overmix.

Arrange overlapping pear slices on the bottom of the cake tin. Reserve the juices from the cooked pears. Spoon the cake mixture over the pears and smooth with a spatula. Bake for 40 minutes or until a toothpick comes out clean when inserted into the middle of the cake. Transfer to a rack and cool for 15 minutes. Run a knife around the edges of the pan to loosen the cake. Place a plate over the cake tin and quickly invert the tin to release the cake. Drizzle the reserved juices over the cake. Serve warm or at room temperature.

Serves 8–10

ICED PAVLOVA

An iced version of the famous dessert. You can make it in advance and just churn it out!

Meringue
2 large egg whites
120g (4 oz) caster sugar
½ teaspoon cornflour (cornstarch)
½ teaspoon vinegar

Ice-cream
4 yolks from medium-sized eggs
1 large egg
120g (4 oz) caster sugar
85g (3 oz) unsalted butter, diced
1 ripe medium-sized mango, stoned, chopped and diced
Pulp from 5 passion fruit
4–5 strawberries, stemmed and diced
210ml (7 fl oz) double cream, chilled

Preheat the oven to 100ºC (210ºF).

Whisk the egg whites until stiff. Add half the sugar and continue to whisk until it looks a little shiny. Fold in the remaining sugar, the cornflour and vinegar.

Use a tablespoon to drop dollops of the meringue mixture onto a greased and parchment paper-lined baking sheet. Bake for one hour, turn off the heat and cool in the oven for 20 minutes. Set aside.

Place the egg yolks, egg and sugar in a mixing bowl and whisk over a pan of simmering water until the mixture thickens. Add the diced butter a little at a time until well mixed. Add in the fruit and mix well.

Crush the meringues slightly with your hand or a fork. Whisk the cream until stiff then fold in the egg mixture and the crushed meringues, mixing well to evenly distribute the ingredients.

Transfer the mixture to an airtight container and freeze until set. After one hour, stir the mixture so the fruits do not settle to the bottom.

Serve with some ginger or shortbread cookies (recipes on page 175).

Makes about 8 portions

GIRLS' NIGHT BREAD-AND-BUTTER PUDDING

I don't know where the original recipe came from — it was shared by Ina on one of our many Wednesday girls'-night dinners. It is a firm favourite.

2 tablespoons unsalted butter, softened
(for greasing the dish)
1 litre (2 pints) heavy cream
60ml (2 fl oz) brandy
2 tablespoons pure vanilla extract
About 300g (11 oz) day-old French (or similar type)
bread or 1 baguette, cut into 1 inch cubes
3 large eggs
250g (8¾ oz) sugar

Topping
110g (4 oz) pecan pieces, toasted
110g (4 oz) firmly packed light brown sugar
½ tablespoon ground cinnamon
2 tablespoons unsalted butter, melted
½ cup pure maple syrup [optional]

Preheat the oven to 160°C (320°F). Butter a large baking dish.

In a large bowl, combine the cream, brandy and vanilla. Add the bread and stir to coat. Put the eggs and sugar in a bowl and use an electric mixer on medium speed to beat until thickened, about five minutes; the mixture should form thick ribbons when the beaters are lifted from the bowl. Mix the eggs and sugar into the bread mixture, then transfer the pudding to the buttered dish.

For the topping, in a small bowl, mix the pecan pieces, brown sugar, cinnamon and butter until thoroughly combined. Spread the topping evenly over the top of the pudding.

Place the baking dish on the middle rack of the oven. Set a larger baking pan filled with a few inches of hot water on the rack beneath. Bake for 55–60 minutes, or until the pudding is set in the centre (it will be slightly jiggly). Remove the pudding from the oven to a wire rack and cool for one hour.

Before serving, drizzle with the maple syrup, if desired.

Serves 6–8

LITTLE GLAZED SUMMER ZABAIONE PUDDINGS

A slight twist to the original British pudding — the *zabaione* makes it all the more delectable!

6 individual serving ramekins

120g (4 oz) raspberries
150g (5 oz) strawberries, chopped to a similar size as the raspberries
150g (5 oz) blueberries or blackberries
A small handful of other mixed berries, redcurrants and blackcurrants [optional]
30–60g (1–2 oz) icing (powdered) sugar
150ml (5 fl oz) sweet white wine
12 slices of sandwich bread, crusts removed

Zabaione
3 yolks from medium-sized eggs
90g (3 oz) caster sugar
4 tablespoon *crème de framboise* or 150ml (5 fl oz) sweet white wine

Wash the fruit, drain and pat dry. Place the fruit — except for the raspberries — with the wine in a saucepan, along with 30g of icing (powdered) sugar. Bring to a simmer and cook for five minutes then stir in the raspberries and cook for one minute on low heat. The idea is not to stew the fruit but keep it firm. The sugar and wine will become a mild syrup. Taste the syrup and add more sugar, if needed. Leave the fruit to cool in the syrup.

Cut the bread into discs to fit the ramekins. Soak the bread slices in the syrup and place at the bottom of the ramekins. Divide half the fruit and syrup between the ramekins. Add another layer of sliced bread then top with the remaining fruit. Refrigerate until ready to serve, up to three days.

To make the *zabaione*, mix the egg yolks, caster sugar, *crème de framboise* and wine in a bowl over a pan of simmering water (*bain marie*), whisking constantly until it thickens and doubles in volume. Spoon over each pudding. Use a torch to give it a burnt glaze and serve immediately.

Note: For a less stodgy pudding, you may put one layer of bread disc instead of two, in each ramekin.

Serves 6

WHITE CHOCOLATE CAKES WITH WHITE CHOCOLATE CREAM CHEESE FROSTING

For lovers of cupcakes and white chocolate with a hint of coconut — these are for you!

Cakes
240g (8 oz) high-quality white chocolate
(such as Lindt or Perugina), chopped
220g (8 oz) plain (all-purpose) flour
1 teaspoon baking powder
½ teaspoon coarse kosher salt
200g (7 oz) sugar
180g (6 oz) unsalted butter, room temperature
1 tablespoon vanilla extract
120ml (4 fl oz) canned unsweetened coconut milk
3 large egg whites

Frosting
140g (5 oz) high-quality white chocolate, chopped
180g (6 oz) cream cheese, at room temperature
6 tablespoons unsalted butter
30g (1 oz) icing (powdered) sugar
½ teaspoon vanilla extract
¼ teaspoon coarse kosher salt

Preheat the oven to 160°C (320°F).

Line three muffin pans (holding six muffins each) with paper liners.

Place the white chocolate in a metal bowl set over a pan of barely simmering water. Stir until melted and smooth.

Whisk the flour, baking powder and salt in a medium bowl. Using an electric mixer, beat the sugar, butter and vanilla in a large bowl until blended. Add the hot white chocolate to the sugar mixture; stir to combine. Add the flour mixture in three additions, alternating with the coconut milk in two additions, beating the batter between additions just to combine.

Using clean dry beaters, beat the egg whites in a medium bowl until they form soft peaks. Gently fold the egg white into the batter in three additions.

Divide the batter evenly between the muffin cups (about ¼ cup each). Bake until a tester inserted into the centre of a cake comes out clean, about 25 minutes. Cool completely. (The cakes can be made one day in advance. Store them in an airtight container at room temperature.)

For the frosting, stir the white chocolate in a metal bowl set over a pan of barely simmering water until melted and smooth. Cool slightly. Using an electric mixer, beat the cream cheese, butter, sugar, vanilla and salt in a medium bowl until fluffy. Gradually beat in the melted white chocolate. Let it cool until thickened to a spreadable consistency. Spread the frosting over the cakes.

Makes 18 cakes

ROAST PEACHES WITH CARAMEL SAUCE

When peaches are in season, they are heavenly. When roasted, the velvety texture and fragrant taste of the fruit complement the sweet nutty caramel.

270g (9 oz) caster sugar, divided
360ml (12 fl oz) orange juice
1 vanilla pod
120g (4 oz) whole pistachios
75g (2½ oz) whole almonds
4 medium whole peaches
60 g (2 oz) raspberries
60g (2 oz) unsalted butter, softened until a little runny but not melting

Put 150g (5 oz) of the sugar with 3 tablespoons water in a heavy-based saucepan and dissolve over a low heat. When the sugar syrup is completely clear, increase the heat and cook for about five minutes or until it forms a light caramel.

Remove from the heat and carefully stir in the orange juice (it will splatter). Do not be disheartened if the caramel hardens, just keep on stirring until the hard bits blend into the sauce. Slit open the vanilla pod, scrape out the seeds and add them to the caramel sauce. Set aside to cool until thickened, then stir in the nuts.

Preheat the oven to 170ºC (340ºF).

Use a blowtorch to blacken the skin of the peaches then use a clean cloth to wipe away the burnt skins. Halve the peaches and discard the pits.

Use a pastry brush to coat the peaches generously with butter. Sprinkle them with the remaining sugar, making sure they are thoroughly coated.

Place the peaches round side up in a small roasting tin. Roast uncovered for 30 minutes, or until the peaches are softened but still intact. Baste them with the pan juices every 10 minutes or so. Add the raspberries and nuts to the roasting tin for the last 10 minutes. Remove from the oven, cover them loosely with foil and leave to cool.

When ready to serve, place a half peach onto individual plates, add some raspberries and spoon the caramel sauce and nuts from the roasting tin over the peach. Serve with a scoop of vanilla or coconut ice-cream (recipe follows on next page).

Serves 8

ROAST PEACHES WITH CARAMEL SAUCE, cont'd

COCONUT ICE-CREAM
1 litre (35 fl oz) whole milk or single cream
9 yolks from medium-sized eggs
210g (7 oz) caster sugar
210ml (7 fl oz) Malibu (Caribbean rum with coconut)

Bring the milk (or cream) to a boil in a saucepan. Whisk the egg yolks and sugar in a bowl until thick. Whisk a little of the hot milk into the egg mixture then pour this into the remaining milk in the saucepan. Cook over low heat, stirring constantly until the custard thickens enough to coat the back of the wooden spoon. Strain and allow to cool.

Stir the Malibu into the cooled custard, then churn in an ice-cream machine. Freeze until firm.

COCONUT BURNT CREAM WITH PINEAPPLE

The classic duo of pineapple and coconut is one of the best — this is no exception! Make this dessert in advance and glaze just before serving.

3 yolks from medium-sized eggs
420ml (14 fl oz) condensed milk
300ml (10 fl oz) milk
90g (3 oz) desiccated coconut
1 tablespoon rum [optional]
Thinly sliced pineapple pieces, dried a little on a paper towel
Caster sugar for dusting

Preheat the oven to 230°C (450°F).

Whisk the egg yolks with the condensed milk. Add the milk, rum and desiccated coconut. Let it rest for 10 minutes then sieve the mixture so that you filter out most of the coconut; discard the filtered coconut bits.

Place eight 10cm (4 inch) ramekins in a roasting tray. Fill the ramekins with the custard cream mixture making sure any coconut bits are evenly distributed. Pour warm water into the roasting tray to come halfway up the sides of the ramekins.

Bake for 12–15 minutes, or until the cream is set. Remove from the oven and cool to room temperature, then refrigerate. Remove from the fridge about 30 minutes before serving.

When ready to serve, arrange a layer of the thinly sliced pineapple pieces over the custard. Sprinkle a thin, even layer of caster sugar over the pineapple. Torch the sugar until the pineapple is glazed beautifully with some burnt edges. Serve immediately.

Serves 8

"SAME WEIGHT" FRESH FRUIT CAKE

The idea is so simple and it works exceptionally well. You simply weigh the eggs and make sure all the other ingredients weigh the same — it couldn't be easier.

3 or 4 eggs – weigh the whole eggs in the shells and note the weight
Flour – same weight as the eggs
Sugar – same weight as the eggs
Butter – same weight as the eggs, at room temperature
Zest of 1 lemon
Juice of half a lemon
150g (5 oz) blueberries or 3 whole seasonal fruit of choice
– e.g. peaches, pears, apples – peeled, cored, sliced
1 teaspoon pure vanilla essence
A pinch of salt

Preheat the oven to 180°C (350°F).

Butter a 25cm (10 inch) round cake pan and line the bottom with a round parchment or wax paper.

Separate the eggs. Cream the butter and sugar at medium-high speed until pale and fluffy, 3–5 minutes. Beat in the egg yolks one at a time. Beat in the lemon juice, zest and vanilla until thoroughly combined. Reduce mixer speed to low and add the sifted flour.

In a separate bowl, beat the egg whites until stiff. Add a pinch of salt.

Stir about one-third of the whites into the cake mixture to lighten it then gently but thoroughly fold in the remaining whites. Scrape the batter into the pan. Sprinkle with the blueberries or the seasonal fruit of choice; press the fruit down slightly.

Bake 30–40 minutes or until a wooden pick or skewer in centre of cake comes out clean. When the cake is done place the pan on a cooling rack. Sprinkle with caster sugar before serving.

Serves 6–8

WHITE CHOCOLATE, CRANBERRY AND MACADAMIA NUT COOKIES

A sweet and delicious combination — great for the holidays!

375g (14 oz) plain (all-purpose) flour
1 teaspoon baking soda
¾ teaspoon salt
240g (8 oz) unsalted butter, room temperature
220g (7½ oz) (packed) golden brown sugar
150g (5 oz) sugar
2 large eggs
1 tablespoon vanilla extract
180g (6 oz) dried cranberries
240g (8 oz) white chocolate chips
130g (4½ oz) coarsely chopped roasted, salted macadamia nuts

Preheat the oven to 180°C (350°F).

Line two large rimmed baking sheets with parchment paper. Sift the first three ingredients into a medium bowl. Use an electric mixer to beat the butter until fluffy. Add both sugars and beat until blended. Beat in the eggs, one at a time, then the vanilla. Add the dry ingredients and mix just until blended. Use a spatula to stir in the cranberries, white chocolate chips and nuts.

For large cookies, drop the dough by heaping tablespoonfuls onto the prepared sheets, spacing them 6cm (2½ inch) apart. For small cookies, drop the dough by level tablespoonfuls onto the sheets, spacing them 3.5cm (1½ inch) apart.

Bake the cookies until just golden, about 18 minutes for large cookies and about 15 minutes for small cookies. Cool on sheets. Store in an airtight container at room temperature up to two days, or freeze up to two weeks.

Makes 36 large or 72 small cookies

KAZI'S CINNAMON SWIRLS

Another recipe from my great friend Kaz. Often baked and waiting for us as we come off the slopes in Whistler. Nothing is better than a batch of these warm out of the oven.

250g (9 oz) plain (all-purpose) flour
2 tablespoons baking powder
A pinch of salt
½ teaspoon cream of tartar
240g (8 oz) softened butter
160ml (5½ oz) milk
50g (1½ oz) brown sugar mixed with 2 teaspoons cinnamon
60g (2 oz) cup white sugar

Preheat the oven to 220°C (425°F).

Add white sugar, flour, baking powder, salt and cream of tartar to the bowl and blend in 120g (4 oz) softened butter until it resembles cookie crumbs. Add the milk, mix and knead gently to create a soft dough. Don't over-knead.

On a lightly floured work surface, roll out the dough into a 1cm thick, 40 x 25cm (15½ x 10 inch) rectangle.

Use a palette knife or flat-bladed knife to spread the remaining 120g (½ cup) of softened butter all over the dough. Sprinkle with brown sugar and cinnamon then roll the dough tightly (like a Swiss roll). Cut the roll into pieces approximately 2cm (¾ inch) wide. Place on a baking sheet and bake for ten minutes or until golden.

Makes about 20

APPLE CRUMBLE ICE-CREAM

A great cold dessert for the lovers of this classic pudding!

Crumble
150g (5 oz) plain (all-purpose) flour
120g (4 oz) unsalted butter, chilled
and cut into small cubes
50g (2 oz) Demerara sugar
50g (2 oz) almonds, chopped

Sauce Anglaise
8 egg yolks
90g (3 oz) caster sugar
300ml (10 fl oz) milk
300ml (10 fl oz) double cream
1 vanilla pod, split

Ice-cream
4 large apples, peeled and cored
180g (6 oz) castor sugar
Juice of 1 lemon

A knob of butter
4 tablespoons *crème fraiche*
2 tablespoons natural yoghurt

Preheat the oven to 200ºC (400ºF)

Rub the butter into the flour until it resembles breadcrumbs, then add the sugar and almonds. Rub again until the mixture becomes a coarse crumb. Sprinkle the mixture onto a baking tray and bake for 15–20 minutes until crunchy and golden brown. Remove from the oven and let it cool. Keep it in airtight container until ready to use.

Dice the apples into 5cm (2 inch) cubes. Melt the butter in a large saucepan. Put in the apples, sugar and the lemon juice. Cook until tender on a medium heat until the apples just start to break up. Spoon away about two-thirds of the apple and liquidise to a smooth puree. Reserve the rest of the apple pieces.

Now mix the puree together with the *crème fraiche* and the yoghurt, churn in an ice-cream machine for about 25 minutes. Let it set in a container in the freezer.

To make the sauce Anglaise, beat the egg yolks and sugar together in a mixing bowl until thick and creamy. Meanwhile, heat the milk and cream together in a saucepan together with the vanilla pod, bringing it to the boil, then let it cool and remove the vanilla pod. Sit the bowl of the egg mixture over a pan of simmering water and whisk in the boiled cream. Then whisk until the custard thickens and coats the back of a wooden spoon. Take off the heat and let it cool. You may reheat gently but do not over-cook or it will be scrambled!

When ready to serve, warm up the apple chunks slightly, scoop out the ice-cream into a serving bowl, spoon some warm apple chunks over the ice-cream. Then sprinkle the crumble over the pudding, followed by some hot custard sauce.

Serves 4–6

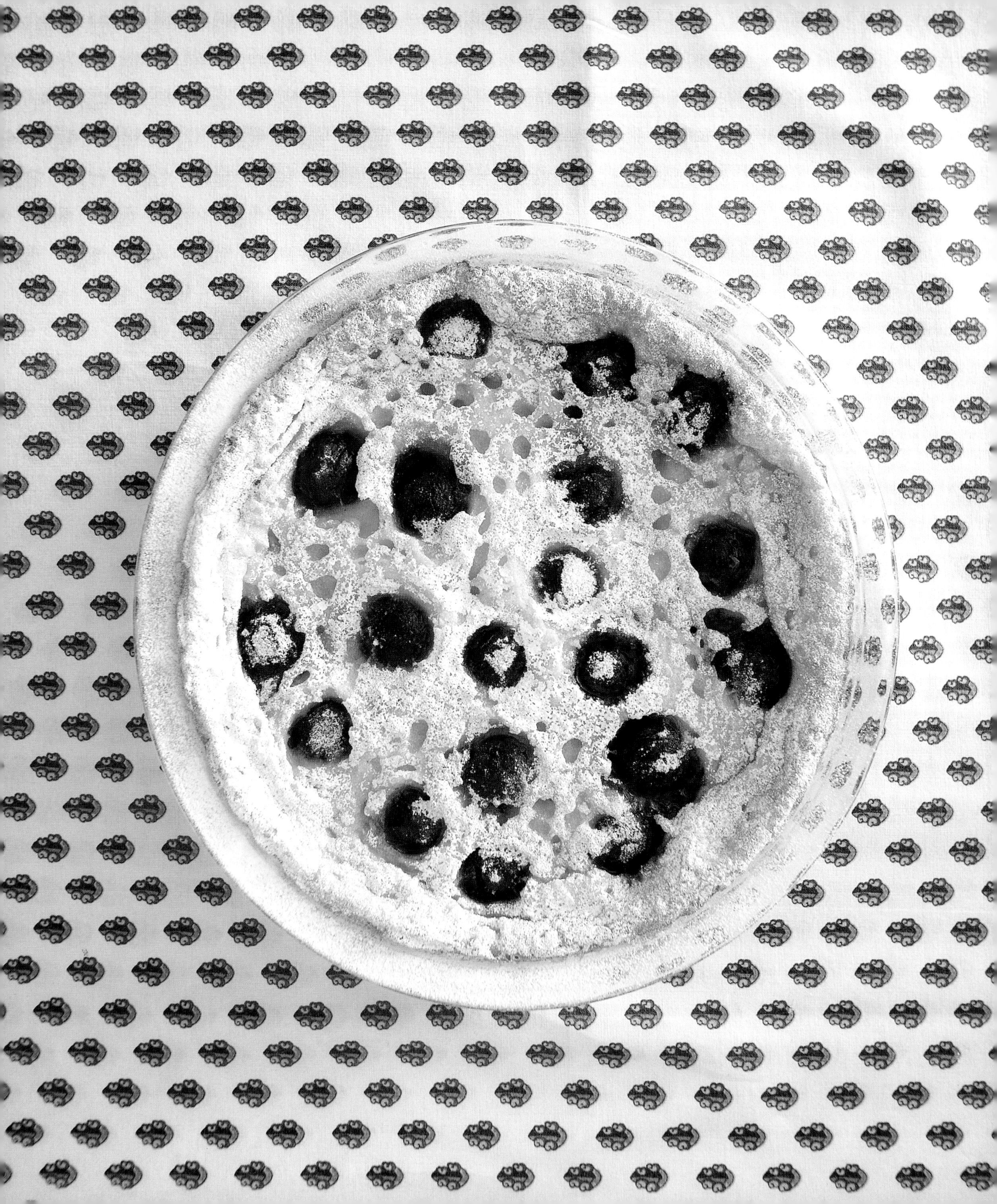

GRANDMA'S CHERRY CLAFOUTI

This is my husband's favourite, although he prefers it without any fruit at all!

500g (17 oz) cherries
120g (4 oz) plain (all-purpose) flour
4 large eggs
250 ml (8½ fl oz) whole milk
1 teaspoon baking powder
25g (1 oz) unsalted butter (melted)
2 tablespoons room temperature butter, plus extra for buttering the baking dish
90g (3 oz) sugar, plus extra for sprinkling

Preheat the oven to 180°C (350°F).

Mix the flour, eggs, milk, baking powder, melted butter and sugar in a bowl until well combined. Butter a medium-sized pie dish. Wash and dry the cherries, then pit them if desired. Place the cherries into the baking dish.

Pour the clafouti mixture on top of the cherries, dot with remaining two tablespoons butter and bake for 30 minutes or until golden. Sprinkle with sugar and serve.

Note: Any fruit can be substituted for the cherries. Ripe pears and peaches are wonderful, as well.

Serves 6–10

SCRUMPTIOUS CHOCOLATE DELIGHTS

Another delicious choco delight for the family — it just cannot go wrong!

170g (6 oz) dark chocolate
120g (4 oz) butter at room temperature
210g (7 oz) caster sugar
2 medium-sized eggs
60g (2 oz) plain (all-purpose) flour, sifted together with ½ teaspoon baking powder
A pinch of salt
1 teaspoon vanilla essence

Icing
150g (5 oz) icing (powdered) sugar
45ml (1½ fl oz) double cream
1 tablespoon cocoa powder
30g (1 oz) butter

Preheat the oven to 180°C (350°F).

Stirring frequently, melt the chocolate in a bowl set over simmering water and set aside when it's completely smooth. Cream the butter and sugar until light and fluffy. Add the eggs one at a time. Stir in the chocolate, mixing well. Fold in the flour, baking powder and salt, then add the vanilla essence.

Butter and lightly flour a 20cm (8 inch) square cake tin. Pour the mixture evenly into the tin. Bake for 30 minutes, or until done. Remove from the oven and cool.

To make the icing, put all the ingredients together in a saucepan and heat slowly, stirring constantly until warm. Let it cool then beat well until smooth.

Spread the icing evenly over the baked chocolate delight. Cool in the refrigerator. When ready to serve, carefully use a palette knife to turn out the delight then cut it into even squares and serve.

Makes about 16–24 squares

RASPBERRY SWIRL CHEESECAKES

Beautiful to look at as well as absolutely delicious!

Approximately 10 (1 cup) finely ground Oreo biscuits (including filling)
40g (1½ oz) unsalted butter melted
150g (5 oz) raspberries (thawed if using frozen)
2 tablespoons icing (powdered) sugar, sifted
375g (13 oz) cream cheese, at room temperature
210g (7 oz) caster sugar
3 large eggs
1 teaspoon vanilla extract

Preheat the oven to 170°C (325°F).

Line a pan for 12 muffins with paper cases. Mix the ground Oreos with the butter in a bowl, divide among the paper cases and press down well. Bake for five minutes then remove from the oven and cool.

Mash the raspberries to a pulp with the back of a fork. Strain through a sieve into a bowl, pressing down well, then discard the seeds. Stir the icing (powdered) sugar into the raspberry pulp.

Place the cream cheese into the bowl of an electric mixer and beat until light and fluffy. Add the caster sugar in a slow, steady stream, beating until combined. Add the eggs one at the time, beating well after each addition, then beat in the vanilla.

Pour the cheese mixture over the Oreo bases. Place small drops (about ½ teaspoon at a time) of berry purée on top and use a wooden skewer to carefully swirl through the cheese mixture.

Bake for 10–15 minutes or until just set. Open the oven door and allow the cakes to cool completely in the switched-off oven.

Makes 12

CHAMPAGNE LEMON SYLLABUB

A variation on the classic English summer sweet — what better way to use up some leftover champagne and biscuits at home!

6–8 wine glasses

6 shortbread biscuits, crushed (bought or homemade, see recipe on page 175)
300ml (10 fl oz) double cream, chilled
60g (2 oz) sugar
150ml (5 fl oz) champagne
Finely grated zest of ½ lemon
About 45ml (1½ fl oz) lemon juice

Some almond flakes or crumble (see page 141 for recipe from apple crumble ice-cream)

Line the bottom of each glass with some crushed shortbread biscuits.

Mix together the double cream, sugar, champagne, lemon zest and some of the juice. Taste the mixture for acidity; it might not need all the lemon juice. Whisk until it resembles softly whipped cream, but without holding peaks. Carefully spoon the cream into the glasses over the crushed biscuits. Chill for at least six hours or overnight.

When ready to serve, sprinkle some almond flakes or crumble on top and add a sprig of mint. Serve it with one or two home-made ginger biscuits (see recipe on page 175).

Serves 6–8

TRUFFLE CAKE

An amazingly easy cake to make — and always impressive!

450g (1 lb) best-quality plain dark chocolate
5 tablespoons liquid glucose
5 tablespoons rum
600ml (20 fl oz) double cream, chilled
120g (4 oz) Amaretti biscuits
Hazelnut or walnut oil, to grease the cake tin

Cocoa powder or chocolate flakes, for dusting
Chilled single cream

Line the base of a 20cm (8 inch) loose-based cake tin with a circle of greaseproof paper. Brush the base and the sides with the oil.

Finely crush the Amaretti biscuits with a rolling pin, then sprinkle them evenly over the bottom of the baking tin.

Break the chocolate into small pieces. Place the chocolate in a bowl with the glucose and rum and heat over a pan of simmering water. Stir until melted and smooth. Remove from the heat and cool for five minutes.

Beat the double cream until slightly thickened then fold half of it into the chocolate mixture. Fold this mixture back into the rest of the cream and mix until well-blended. Spoon into the tin and tap the tin to smooth out the top. Cover with cling film and chill overnight.

When ready to serve, run a palette knife around the edge to loosen the cake then remove the tin. Sprinkle some cocoa powder or chocolate flakes over the surface and serve with chilled single cream.

Serves 8

LITTLE LEMON SOUFFLÉS

Soufflés **always make people nervous. These are practically foolproof! To make them even easier, forget the lemon shells and bake in individual ramekins.**

8 large lemons
3 large eggs, separated
100g (4 oz) sugar
2 tablespoons plain (all-purpose) flour
Icing (powdered) sugar, for dusting

Preheat the oven to 180°C (350°F).

Trim the ends of each lemon so the fruit sits level. Cut off the opposite end one-third of the way down, parallel with the bottom. Reserve the tops.

Working over a sieve set over a bowl, scoop the pulp from the lemons, being careful to keep the shell intact. Squeeze the pulp over a bowl and reserve the juice. Place the lemon shells on a baking sheet lined with parchment paper.

Put the yolks, half the sugar, 60ml (2 fl oz) lemon juice and the flour in a heatproof bowl and whisk with an electric mixer until pale, about three minutes.

Set the bowl over a pan of simmering water and whisk until the mixture is very thick, about six minutes. Remove the bowl from the heat and beat on medium speed until cooled, about 10 minutes. Set aside.

Put the egg whites and the remaining sugar into a clean bowl set over a pan of simmering water. Whisk until the sugar has dissolved and the mixture is warm. Remove the bowl from the heat and beat on low heat until foamy. Gradually increase the speed, beating until the meringue is shiny and holds soft peaks, about 2–3 minutes.

Whisk one-third of the meringue into the lemon mixture. Use a rubber spatula to gently fold in the remaining meringue. Fill the prepared shells up to the rim. Bake until the filling is slightly golden and rises about 2.5cm (1 inch) above the rim, 16–18 minutes. Dust with icing (powdered) sugar and garnish with the reserved lemon tops, if desired. Serve immediately.

Makes 8 soufflés

SWEET BEANPASTE PANCAKE

An all-time favourite yet so few people realise it is so simple to make!

3 medium-sized eggs
150g (5 oz) wheat flour
240ml (8 fl oz) cold water
240g (8 oz) sweet red beanpaste or ground dates
1.4 litres (3 pints) cooking oil

Beat the eggs in a mixing bowl then add the flour and cold water. Mix well until it becomes a loose batter.

Heat a 15cm (6 inch) flat frying pan and lightly coat it with oil. Pour in one-fourth of the batter, or just enough to lightly coat the bottom of the pan. Cook on low heat for a few seconds or until set, then remove from the pan — do not cook the other side. Repeat with the remaining batter to form four pancakes.

Place a pancake on a board with the uncooked side up. Add one-fourth of the beanpaste in the centre and spread into a rectangle of about 12 x 5cm (5 x 2 inch). Fold the bottom edge of the pancake up first, fold the left and right sides toward the centre, making an envelope. Brush the top edge of the pancake with some flour batter and fold it down so it adheres.

Heat the oil until hot. Deep fry the pancakes until golden and crisp, about two minutes.

Remove from the oil, drain and cut each pancake into six or seven slices. Serve immediately.

Makes 4 pancakes

MAMINE'S CRÈME CARAMEL

This recipe comes from my mother-in-law and I think it's the best one I have had. It never fails to please — especially my children.

Custard
4 large eggs
100g (3½ oz) white sugar
½ teaspoon vanilla extract
4 sachets vanilla sugar (about 4 tablespoons)
500ml (16¾ fl oz) whole milk

Caramel
240ml (8 fl oz) water
100g (3½ oz) white sugar

A 25cm (10 inch) glass pie dish at least 5cm (2 inch) deep.

Place a rack in the middle of the oven and preheat the oven to 180°C (350°F).

To make the caramel, heat 240ml (8 oz) water and 100g (½ cup) sugar in a non-stick pan until the sugar melts and becomes a deep golden caramel colour. Immediately pour the caramel into the pie dish and tilt to coat the bottom and sides evenly.

To make the custard, combine the milk, white sugar and vanilla sugar in a saucepan and bring to a simmer; remove from the heat.

Whisk the eggs together in a bowl and then slowly add the hot milk mixture, whisking constantly. Pour the custard into the pie plate.

Put the pie plate in a baking pan. Add enough hot water to the pan to reach halfway up the side of the pie dish. Bake the custard until it is set but still trembles slightly, 40–45 minutes (it will continue to set as it cools). Remove the pie dish from the water and let it cool completely.

Cover the custard loosely with plastic wrap and refrigerate for at least two hours. Run a knife around the edge of the *crème caramel* and gently shake the pie dish back and forth to make sure the custard is loosened. Invert a serving plate on top of the pie dish then invert the *crème caramel* onto it — the caramel will run out to the edges of the plate.

Serves 6–10

MARMALADE JELLY WITH CHOCOLATE COULIS

The refreshing marmalade jelly texture goes perfectly with the thin dark-chocolate topping! A childhood favourite, with a modern twist.

8 mini jelly cups or dessert wine glasses

Jelly
120g (4 oz) thin-cut Seville orange marmalade
150ml (5 fl oz) water
360ml (12 fl oz) fresh orange juice, strained
120g (4 oz) caster sugar
4 gelatine leaves

Chocolate coulis
120g (4 oz) dark chocolate
45g (1½ oz) butter
60g (2 oz) sugar
60ml (2 fl oz) water

Bring the marmalade, water, orange juice and sugar to the boil in a saucepan. Meanwhile, soak the gelatine leaves in cold water. Once the gelatine is soft, drain and squeeze the leaves to remove excess moisture. Add the gelatine to the marmalade mixture, stir until it is dissolved, then pour straight into the cups or glasses.

Allow to cool at room temperature before refrigerating until set, at least 1–2 hours.

Prepare the chocolate coulis. In a saucepan, melt the dark chocolate, butter and sugar over low heat until smooth. Stir in the water to make a smooth, thick cream. Just before serving, pour a thin layer of the chocolate over the jelly; it will set as a topping. Decorate with a sprig of mint and some crushed nuts.

Serves 8

CHOCOLATE-TO-THE-MAX COOKIES

Chocolate, chocolate and more chocolate — definitely for those addicted to the taste of chocolate!

165g (6 oz) firmly packed dark brown sugar
200g (7 oz) sugar
200g (7 oz) unsalted butter, softened
1 teaspoon vanilla extract
2 large-sized eggs
260g (9 oz) plain (all-purpose) flour
100g (4 oz) Dutch or Belgian cocoa
1 teaspoon baking powder
½ teaspoon salt
100g (4 oz) dark (semi-sweet) chocolate, finely chopped
100g (4 oz) milk chocolate, finely chopped

Preheat the oven to 180°C (350°F).

Use an electric mixer to beat the sugars, butter and vanilla until pale and fluffy. Add the eggs one at a time, beating after each addition. Sift the flour, cocoa powder, baking powder and salt and add to the mixture.

Add the dark and milk chocolates and stir to combine. Scoop half-tablespoons of the mixture, shape into balls and place onto paper-lined baking trays. Flatten slightly with the palm of your hand and bake for eight minutes. Cool on trays.

Makes 4–6 dozen cookies

TARTY TREACLE TART

A great all-time classic pudding. It travels well, so you can take it to friends or on boat trips!

A 23cm (9 inch) loose-based tart tin, greased

Pastry
240g (8 oz) plain (all-purpose) flour
120g (4 oz) unsalted butter, chilled and cut into small cubes
1 medium-sized egg

Filling
450g (15 oz) golden syrup
90g (3 oz) fresh white breadcrumbs
¼ teaspoon ground ginger
Finely grated zest of one lemon
2 tablespoons lemon juice
Cold milk, for brushing

Sieve the flour and rub in the butter until it resembles coarse breadcrumbs. Add the egg and mix well with a wooden spoon. Knead the mixture into a dough, cover with plastic wrap and refrigerate for about 30 minutes.

Roll out two-thirds of the pastry on a lightly floured board and line the tart tin. Prick the base with a fork and leave to rest in fridge for 30 minutes — this will prevent the tart base from shrinking when baking. Keep the remaining dough in the fridge.

Preheat the oven to 190ºC (375ºF).

Mix together the golden syrup, breadcrumbs, ginger, lemon zest and juice and leave to thicken for at least 10 minutes. Pour into the pastry case.

Roll out the remaining dough and cut into strips that are 1cm (⅓ inch) wide. Lay the strips in a lattice pattern on top of the tart. Brush a little milk onto the end of each strip and press onto the edge of the tart to help it adhere. Brush a little milk over the strips, then bake the tart in the middle of the oven for 30 minutes. Serve the tart warm or cold with some whipped cream.

Serves 8

CHOCOLATE PEAR POTS

Ginger, chocolate and pears — a wonderful combination. If, however, you don't like ginger, just omit it!

3 ripe pears
Juice of half a lemon
200g (7 oz) sugar, divided
2 tablespoons honey
1cm (½ inch) piece of fresh ginger, finely chopped
½ teaspoon cinnamon
200g (7 oz) dark chocolate (70% cacao)
500ml (16¾ fl oz) whole milk
5 egg yolks
1 whole egg
2 tablespoons *crème fraiche*

Preheat the oven to 180°C (350°F).

Peel the pears, cut them into small cubes and mix with the lemon juice. Place the pears in a saucepan with 150g (5 oz) sugar, the honey, ginger and cinnamon. Cook on a low fire until very soft and the liquid is transparent. Filter the juices from the pears and set the pears aside. Boil the pear juices until syrupy.

Remix the syrup into the pears and leave to cool.

Melt the chocolate with the milk, either in a bowl over simmering water or carefully in the microwave. In the meantime, beat the egg yolks, egg, and the remaining 50g (1½ oz) sugar and *crème fraiche*. Add the chocolate/milk mixture.

Divide the pear mixture into eight little glasses or ramekins and slowly pour the chocolate mixture on top until about 1cm (¼ inch) below the brim.

Place the ramekins into a baking dish with hot water that comes at least halfway up the sides of the ramekins. Carefully place in the oven and bake for 30 minutes. The water should not be boiling as the chocolate pots need to cook slowly to keep their creaminess.

Cook at least 1 hour and cover with plastic cling film until ready to serve. Before serving, top with a dollop of *crème fraiche* or whipped cream if desired.

Serves 8

SIMPLY WONDERFUL HOMEMADE BISCUITS

I have been asked so many times for these biscuit recipes. They are so wonderfully simple and so simply wonderful!

SHORTBREAD BISCUITS

120g (4 oz) unsalted butter, at room temperature
60g (2 oz) caster sugar, plus extra for dusting
180g (6 oz) plain (all-purpose) flour

Preheat the oven to 150°C (300°F).

Beat the butter until soft then beat in the sugar and mix in the sifted flour. Use a wooden spoon to stir it well then finish mixing the moist dough with your hands. Scrape the dough onto a board or worktop lightly dusted with caster sugar. Roll the dough to about 2mm (⅛ inch) thick. You may want to dust the rolling pin with caster sugar as well. Use biscuit cutters to cut out the biscuits and arrange them on a greased baking tray. Bake on a high shelf in the oven for about 25 minutes, or until done. Cool on a wire rack, dust them again with caster sugar and store in an airtight container.

Makes 20–24 biscuits

GINGER BISCUITS

120g (4 oz) self-raising flour
60g (2 oz) margarine
60g (2 oz) golden syrup

45g (1½ oz) caster sugar
2 teaspoons ginger powder
1 yolk from a medium-sized egg

Preheat the oven to 180°C (350°F).

Melt the margarine with the syrup over low heat. Sieve the flour into a bowl then mix in the ginger powder and sugar. Stir in the margarine and syrup mixture. Beat in the egg yolk thoroughly. Divide the dough into 15 round balls. Flatten each ball and roll to a thickness of 2mm (⅛ inch). Place the biscuits onto a greased baking sheet and bake for about 15 minutes, or until golden. Cool, then store in an airtight container.

These biscuits are great with ice-cream, or simply wonderful on their own.

Makes 15 biscuits

BANANA COFFEE CAKE WITH CHOCOLATE-CHIP STREUSEL

My boys love this. Perfect for afternoon tea and perfect for a picnic outing! Use bananas with some black spots on the skin, which indicates they are really ripe.

240g (8 oz) white chocolate chips
150g (5 oz) (packed) golden brown sugar
60g (2 oz) chopped pecans
190g (7 oz) plain (all-purpose) flour
¾ teaspoon baking soda
¾ teaspoon baking powder
¼ teaspoon salt
150g (5 oz) sugar
120g (4 oz) unsalted butter, room temperature
1 large egg
300g (11 oz) mashed very ripe bananas (about 3 large)
3 tablespoons plain yoghurt

Preheat the oven to 180°C (350°F).

Butter and flour a 20cm (8 inch) square metal baking pan that's 5cm (2 inch) deep. Stir the chocolate chips, brown sugar and pecans in a small bowl until well blended; set the streusel aside.

Sift the flour, baking soda, baking power and salt into a medium bowl. Use an electric mixer to beat the sugar, butter and egg in a large bowl until fluffy. Beat in the mashed bananas and yoghurt. Add the dry ingredients and blend well.

Spread half of batter in the prepared baking pan. Sprinkle with half the streusel. Repeat the layering. Bake until a tester inserted into the centre comes out clean, about 45 minutes. Cool the coffee cake in the pan on a rack.

12 servings

QUICK LEMON MERINGUE TART

An easy recipe to prepare beforehand — just assemble when you need it!

Sweet shortcrust pastry
240g (8 oz) plain (all-purpose) flour
A pinch of salt
150g (5 oz) unsalted butter, chilled
90g (3 oz) caster sugar
1 whole medium to large egg
1 yolk from a medium to large sized egg

Filling
2 whole medium to large eggs
90g (3 oz) caster sugar
Finely grated zest and juice of 1½ lemons
60ml (2 fl oz) double cream

Meringue
2 egg medium to large whites
1 teaspoon white vinegar
120g (4 oz) caster sugar
1 teaspoon cornflour (cornstarch)

Preheat the oven to 200°C (400°F).

Make the pastry. Sift the flour with the salt. Rub in the butter into the flour until the mix resembles coarse breadcrumbs. Stir in the sugar then add the egg yolk and egg. Combine the ingredients to form dough, cover with plastic wrap and refrigerate for about 30 minutes.

Roll the dough on a floured work surface then place in a 23cm (9 inch) loose-based tart tin. Line the pastry with greaseproof paper and raw rice, bake for 10 minutes. When the pastry is firm but uncoloured, remove the greaseproof paper and rice and bake it further for five minutes. Take it out and let it cool.

Turn the oven down to 150°C (300°F). For the filling, whisk all the ingredients together and pour into a bowl. Place in a roasting tray half-filled with warm water and bake for 20 minutes, or until just set. Remove from the oven and let it cool.

Whisk the egg whites and vinegar to soft peaks. Add the sugar and cornflour and whisk to firm peaks. Spoon dollops of the meringue onto a baking sheet which you have lined with paper and greased. Bake for 20 minutes, or until firm. Let cool.

When ready to serve, fill the tart shell with the lemon curd filling, using a palette knife to level it. Arrange the mini meringues attractively on top of the filling and serve.

Serves 8

INDEX

A & B

Apple Crumble Ice-Cream 141
Bacon-Wrapped Baked Chicken
    with Sun-dried Tomatoes 53
Banana Coffee Cake with
    Chocolate-Chip Streusel 177
Beanpaste Pancake, Sweet 159
Beef Daube, Provençal 37
Beef Satay, Satay Sauce & Shrimp
    Sambal Condiment, Kin's 77–78
Beef, Korean 51
Beef with Garlic
    and Sweet Soya Sauce, Tasty 91
Beetroot and Broccoli Salad 61
Biscuits, Simply
    Wonderful Homemade 175
Bread-and-Butter Pudding,
    Girls' Night 115
Brownies, Ultimate Caramel 103–104

C

Cake, "Same Weight" Fresh Fruit 131
Cake, Pear Honey 111
Cake, Truffle 155
Cakes with White Chocolate Cream
Cheese Frosting, White Chocolate 123
Calamari 'Arancia'
    (Orange-Glazed Squid) 73
Caramel Brownies, Ultimate 103–104
Champagne Lemon Syllabub 149
Cheesecakes, Raspberry Swirl 147
Cherry Clafouti, Grandma's 143
Chicken Adobo – Philippine Style 43
Chicken, Shantung 21
Chicken with Basil, Spicy 23
Chicken with Sun-dried Tomatoes,
    Bacon-Wrapped Baked 53
Chocolate Delights, Scrumptious 145
Chocolate Pear Pots 173
Cinnamon Swirls, Kazi's 139
Clafouti, Grandma's Cherry 143
Clams with Garlic and Chilli,
    Steamed 27
Coconut Burnt Cream
    with Pineapple 129
Coconut Ice-Cream 126
Cod with a Fennel and Saffron Sauce 87

Coffee Cake with Chocolate-Chip
    Streusel, Banana 177
Cookies, Chocolate-to-the-Max 165
Cookies, White Chocolate, Cranberry
    and Macadamia Nut 133
Crème Caramel, Mamine's 161

D

Daube, Provençal Beef 37

F & G

Fish Fillets, Provençal 59
Fish Stew, Easy 25
Goat Cheese and Toro Dip 19

I

Ice-Cream, Apple Crumble 141
Ice-Cream, Coconut 126

J & K

Kedgeree, Good Ol' Barbara's 85

L & M

Lamb Loin with Orange
    and Mint Crust 57
Lamb Rack in Miso 35
Lamb Shanks in a Red Wine Sauce,
    Slow-Braised 93
Lemon Meringue Tart,
    Quick 179
Marmalade Jelly
    with Chocolate Coulis 163
Meringue Tart,
    Quick Lemon 179

O & P

Pancake, Sweet Beanpaste 159
Parfait, Passion Fruit 101
Pasta and Roasted Vegetable Gratin 71
Pasta with Corn, Broccolini,
    Peas and Parmesan 39
Pavlova, Iced 113
Peaches with Caramel Sauce,
    Roast 125–126
Pear Honey Cake 111
Pear Pots, Chocolate 173
Pigeon, Roast 69

Pork, Cantonese Steamed Minced 89
Pork, Oma's Roast 75
Pudding, Girls' Night
    Bread-and-Butter 115
Puddings, Little Glazed
    Summer Zabaione 121
Pumpkin Mash 61

Q & R

Quail, Grilled Spiced 41
Raspberry Swirl Cheesecakes 147
Ribs, Asian-Style Barbecued Spare 55

S

Salad, Beetroot and Broccoli 61
Satay Sauce & Shrimp Sambal
    Condiment, Kin's Beef Satay 77–78
Soufflés, Little Lemon 157
Spinach, Sesame 62
Spaghetti with Oriental Ragu 45
Squid, Orange-Glazed
    (Calamari 'Arancia') 73
Stew, Easy Fish 25
Syllabub, Champagne Lemon 149

T & U

Tart, Quick Lemon Meringue 179
Tarte Tatin, Mango 109
Tartlets, Caramelized Banana 99
Tian of Provençal Vegetables 29
Toro and Goat Cheese Dip 19
Treacle Tart, Tarty 167
Truffle Cake 155

V

Veal Meatballs,
    Melt-in-Your-Mouth 67
Veal with Zucchini and Basil 83
Vegetable Trio 61–62

W & Z

White Chocolate Cakes with White
Chocolate Cream Cheese Frosting 123
White Chocolate, Cranberry
    and Macadamia Nut Cookies 133
Zabaione Puddings,
    Little Glazed Summer 121